CONSERVATIVES IN THE PROGRESSIVE ERA

The Taft Republicans of 1912

by Norman M. Wilensky

University of Florida Monographs

SOCIAL SCIENCES

No. 25, Winter 1965

UNIVERSITY OF FLORIDA PRESS / GAINESVILLE, FLORIDA

PREFACE

The effect of the reform movement on the Republican party schism of 1912 has attracted the interest of many American historians, but their works have stressed the role of the insurgent-progressives. There is a need for an analysis of regular, conservative Republicanism, and this study examines that important yet neglected force in the Progressive Era.

The major thesis of this study is that President Taft, in alliance with the Republican Old Guard, began a political attack early in 1911 which was primarily responsible for the conservative control of the Republican party at the close of 1912. After the congressional elections of 1910, the Old Guard took the offensive in the struggle for party dominance. Historians of the Progressive period have not recognized the importance of this early Old Guard activity, or of Taft's role in it. They have, on the contrary, emphasized both the inadequacy of the Old Guard political position and the ineptness of the President's leadership. Yet Taft's long-range preparation was largely responsible for his renomination. Several months before the progressives unified their forces, Taft planned a nation-wide tour, to begin in September, 1911, in order to mobilize the Old Guard. The public and the press in 1911 did not understand the President's political intentions, and historians of the Taft Administration have also been unaware of the tour's meaning.

This study also describes, for the first time, the Old Guard leaders and their methods of organization throughout the country. Charles Dewey Hilles, the secretary to the President who captained the Old Guard attack, forged a strategy which overcame much factionalism within the Old Guard as well as the strenuous opposition of Theodore Roosevelt and his supporters. This gave Taft control of convention machinery and provided him with enough delegates to withstand a strong progressive attempt to control the Republican party. Chapter 2 stresses the relationship of Taft's offensive in 1911 to his renomination the next year, while the first chapter is largely background to this theme. Roosevelt's challenge, the Republican convention in June, 1912, and the final weeks of the Old Guard campaign are detailed in the fourth and fifth chapters.

Another theme of this study is that ideology provided the central differentiation between regular and progressive Republicans. This view contrasts with that of Richard Hofstadter, who, in *The Age of Reform: From Bryan to F.D.R.*, stresses dissimilarities in social and economic status as the key factor of the Republican schism. Historians of the Progressive period have, by and large, accepted this thesis. The initial sections of Chapter 3, which present a social and economic profile of nearly 900 Old Guardsmen from every state, show that the Taft men were remarkably similar to their progressive counterparts, and that together these leaders formed the elite of the Republican party. Not status but ideology separated Republicans, and the remaining sections of the third chapter contrast the conservative political thought of the Old Guard with the dominant progressive ideology. Most of the enthusiasm for Taft, which helped greatly to mobilize the regular Republicans against their antagonists, emanated from men with sincere conservative convictions.

I was especially fortunate to be the first person to have access to the Charles Dewey Hilles Papers in the Yale University Library, which served as the major source material for Chapters 2 and 4. Most of this very large collection, reflecting Hilles' political activities as secretary to President Taft and chairman of the Republican National Committee, provided a detailed record of Republican affairs in every state from 1911 to 1913; it also contained those names of Old Guardsmen so vital to the profile presented in Chapter 3.

The William Howard Taft Papers in the Library of Congress were particularly useful for the period 1908-10, with the President's letters to his brothers, Theodore Roosevelt, and Old Guard congressmen sharply revealing his political attitudes.

Of the remaining collections, I found the Henry L. Stimson Papers in the Yale University Library to be the most valuable. Stimson's correspondence explained his part in the New York campaign of 1910, while his "Diary" clearly presented his position on the Taft-Roosevelt split as well as his role in the campaign of 1912. The Charles Nagel Papers and the William Rockwell Sheffield Papers, both at Yale, and the Nicholas Murray Butler Papers at the Columbia University Library contained a number of significant references to the campaign of 1912. The Walter Lionel Pfortzheimer Collection in the Yale University Library contained two folders of Roosevelt correspondence with about a dozen pertinent letters.

In its original form, this study was a doctoral thesis in history at Yale University. Without the constant advice of Professor John Morton Blum it could not have been written, and I am deeply grateful to him. I also wish to acknowledge the generous cooperation and assistance of the staffs of the Historical Manuscripts Division and the Reference Department of the Yale University Library. Finally, I extend my thanks to the Graduate School of the University of Florida for making this publication possible.

NORMAN M. WILENSKY

GAINESVILLE, FLORIDA
FEBRUARY, 1965

CONTENTS

1. THE REPUBLICAN PARTY
IN DIVISION

William Howard Taft was confident that he had a clear mandate from the American people and the Republican party after the presidential election of 1908. When he took office in March, 1909, Taft anticipated an era of political good feeling exceeding the one during Monroe's second administration. Contrary to this expectation, Republicans divided over legislative, ideological, and party matters within two years. By the end of 1910 Taft was a partisan President, deeply involved in political machinations.

Little in the close association between Taft and Theodore Roosevelt had suggested the course of division.[1] As a Cabinet member, an intimate adviser to Roosevelt, and a sort of trouble shooter for the Administration, Taft appeared to be a Roosevelt progressive. Roosevelt exhibited the utmost confidence in him by choosing him as his successor. Certainly Taft thought himself a loyal devotee of Roosevelt. On the major issues of the 1908 campaign—labor, capital, the panic of 1907, currency reform, trusts, railroad regulation, government ownership, socialism, tariff, income tax, and court reform—Taft stood only a fraction to the right of Roosevelt. When the New York newspapers expressed regret that the presidential nominee was defending Roosevelt in his speeches instead of establishing policies of his own, Taft confessed that he did not know what the press had expected him to do. "If my views were so at variance with the Administration's policies, as they seem to have thought in advance," he wrote, "then it is truly remarkable that I could stay in the Cabinet."[2]

Nevertheless, both in temperament and in his political outlook, Taft was markedly different from his former chief. A man of abounding good nature and good intentions, Taft had small knowledge of the problems of the industrial worker or of practical politics. His just mind was

1. While this chapter serves largely as background, and much of the material is not new, it is essential to cover, at least generally, the multiplicity of events in the Republican schism from 1908 to 1910. For the best account of the Taft-Roosevelt split, see G. E. Mowry, *Theodore Roosevelt and the Progressive Movement* (Madison, Wis., 1947).

2. Roosevelt to Taft, July 21, 1908, Taft to Roosevelt, March 21, 1909, William Howard Taft Papers, Library of Congress; Taft to Hilles, September 4, 1907, Charles Dewey Hilles Papers, Yale University Library.

statute-ridden. Although he had talent for certain kinds of public serv-ice, notably for the bench or the administration of a department of government, Taft lacked Roosevelt's dynamic qualities of popular leadership.

Roosevelt and Taft also differed in their views of the presidency and of government. Taft believed wholeheartedly in the constitutional limita-tions of executive power, a concept which Roosevelt never shared. In this, more than in any other single issue, lay the seed of inescapable con-flict. Taft thought that his role was not to initiate policy. By meeting issues on the basis of law, the new President hoped to preserve the guarantees of life, liberty, and property secured by the Constitution.[3]

Once Roosevelt's personality no longer dominated him, Taft began to choose associates on the basis of his conservative inclinations and with-out much regard for practical politics. At the outset of the new Adminis-tration, Taft named seven corporation lawyers to his Cabinet and failed to reappoint Roosevelt's progressive friends, James R. Garfield and Luke E. Wright. Taft explained that he had based his selections on the need for expert legal counsel.[4]

Contact with the progressive Republicans seemed to unnerve the Presi-dent. Gradually he sought the companionship of men like Senator W. Murray Crane of Massachusetts, a strict organization man who distrusted reformers, particularly those in his own party. Increasingly it became Taft's habit to confer with Crane, and as the President drew closer to him and other Old Guard congressmen, he considered less the views and aspirations of the progressives in his party.[5]

Taft's growing reliance on the Old Guard coincided with an insurgent uprising against standpat congressional power. The congressional session of 1909 showed that the Republican party which Taft inherited was already a house divided against itself. In the Senate the hard core of the Old Guard consisted of about ten men, headed by Nelson W. Aldrich of Rhode Island. His leadership rested on a natural talent for managing things and dealing with his colleagues. The other standpatters included Eugene Hale of Maine, Crane and Henry Cabot Lodge of Massachusetts,

3. H. F. Pringle, *The Life and Times of William Howard Taft* (2 vols., New York, 1939), II, 758; W. H. Taft, *Present Day Problems* (New York, 1908), 188-89, 218-19, 289.

4. Although Roosevelt was keenly disappointed, he offered no protest until his split with Taft. Then Roosevelt complained that the quality of Taft's Cabinet was an example of personal disloyalty and conservatism.

5. H. L. Stimson, "Diary," 1910-13, 59, Henry L. Stimson Papers, Yale Uni-versity Library; S. B. Griffin, *W. Murray Crane: A Man and Brother* (Boston, 1926), 186-88; Hilles to Mrs. Hilles, August 12, 1909, Hilles Papers.

Boies Penrose of Pennsylvania, Reed Smoot of Utah, Elihu Root and Chauncey M. Depew of New York, John Kean of New Jersey and Jacob H. Gallinger of New Hampshire. They were opposed by an almost equal block of progressives: Jonathan P. Dolliver and Albert B. Cummins of Iowa, Moses E. Clapp and Knute Nelson of Minnesota, Robert M. La Follette of Wisconsin, Joseph L. Bristow of Kansas, Albert J. Beveridge of Indiana, and Coe Crawford and Robert J. Gamble of South Dakota. At various times other Senators, more pliant and less capable, aided each group. The leaders of the Old Guard in the House were Speaker Joe Cannon of Illinois—who ruled the chamber with an iron hand—James A. Tawney of Minnesota, Herbert Parsons of New York, and William B. McKinley of Illinois. The most effective of the insurgent Republicans were George W. Norris of Nebraska, Victor Murdock of Kansas, Miles Poindexter of Washington, and Augustus P. Gardner of Massachusetts.

The power of the Old Guard was on the wane by 1909. The election of 1908 brought defeat to a number of old-time leaders, while it added strength to the progressive element in both houses. When William B. Allison, John C. Spooner, and Orville H. Platt left the Senate, Aldrich remained as the last of the four men who had dominated that body in the name of high conservatism for so many years. Lodge, Crane, and Hale became Aldrich's most trusted lieutenants, but they were not the equal of the men they replaced. The arrival of new congressmen, particularly from the Middle West, placed Cannon's position in jeopardy. Before the first congressional session of Taft's Administration, as the President knew, the insurgents formulated plans to challenge the authority of Aldrich and Cannon.[6]

Because he thought that the insurgent cause was hopeless, Taft decided to work cooperatively with the Old Guard leadership in Congress. "I have a definite program of legislation which I am bound to push through," the President maintained. "Cannon and Aldrich have promised to stand by the party platform and to follow my lead."[7]

The first fifteen months of the Taft Administration brought to the front the fundamental division in the Republican party. The President's program became enmeshed in a power struggle as time and again Taft saw the insurgent-progressive wing of his party block or alter his proposals. The tariff debate in the Senate and the fight to contain Cannon's rule in the House marked the opening wedge of the estrangement be-

6. Taft to Roosevelt, November 7, 1908, Taft Papers.
7. Taft to Horace Taft, March 16, 1909, and to Theodore Roosevelt, March 21, 1909, Taft Papers.

3

tween Taft and the progressives. Other issues, such as railroad regulation and conservation, followed naturally along the lines of this schism. Their success in debate encouraged the insurgents to fight harder, but the regular Republicans, determined to maintain control over the party machinery, became only more resolute.

Caught between his conservative predilections and his desire to continue the Roosevelt policies, Taft compounded Republican party difficulties and added confusion to the congressional realignment of forces. The President's actions during the tariff fight typified his political vacillation. Taft seemed so shocked at the high rates of the Aldrich bill reported to the Senate in the spring of 1909 that the progressives believed the President would be their ally on this issue. Senator La Follette maintained that Taft told him he would disapprove the measure unless it met with the platform obligations. When the President held a series of conferences with Aldrich and Cannon in May, however, it looked as though he had deserted the progressives. In June Senator Beveridge was so confused that twice he changed his mind as to whether the President was with the progressives or against them. As the Old Guard leadership in the Senate emasculated the tariff in the interest of high rates, progressive Republicans urged the President to fight Aldrich and his schemes. Taft might have challenged the regulars for their disloyalty to himself and the party platform, but to do so he had to join the insurgents, and he had little confidence in them. His course was neither consistent nor effective.

With each debate in Congress hostility increased between the two Republican camps. The progressives felt that the President had betrayed them, while Taft showed his complete annoyance with the insurgents. Taft maintained that whenever he proposed something to carry out reforms, the progressives opposed it because they said it came as a gift from Aldrich. The President commented that the strenuous supporters of Roosevelt, "those who like to call themselves 'progressives,'" were very suspicious of him. They referred to his interviews with Cannon and Aldrich as an indication that he was departing from Roosevelt's policies and consorting with reactionary people. But Taft said privately: "What a fool I would be if I joined, or permitted myself to countenance, the yelping and snarling at Cannon and Aldrich, which these so-called 'progressives' and their amateur political newspaper correspondents are insisting upon as a mark of loyalty to the Roosevelt policies . . . they do not look beyond their noses."[8]

8. Taft to Horace Taft, July 27, 1909, Taft Papers.

Offended that members of his own party were attacking his legislative program, Taft became convinced of the need for organized political authority. Under the exhortation of Old Guard advisers who wished to cleanse the Republican party of insurgency, the President agreed to use his patronage power. In December, 1909, with the House insurgents ready to undermine Speaker Cannon's position, Taft decided that he was going to separate the sheep from the goats. "These gentlemen," he wrote to his friend Otto Bannard, "who profess to be Republicans and will yet do anything to bring the Democratic party into power can not expect me to assist them with patronage, and I hope to make this plain as I can before I get through."[9]

The patronage battle broke in January, 1910, when Cannon told a surprised House that the President would oppose those who wanted to reduce the power of the Speaker. Shortly thereafter the Republican Congressional Campaign Committee, headed by Old Guard Congressman McKinley, announced that it would oppose insurgency in the coming elections and would advocate the nomination and election of regular and loyal Republicans. Postmaster General Frank Hitchcock then confirmed the news that he was holding up post office appointments which the insurgents had recommended. Yet the insurgents continued their struggle against Cannon. The high point of the fight came in March, when they rallied enough Democrats and Republicans to pass the Norris resolution that stripped the Speaker of most of his power.

Taft was greatly disturbed by Cannon's defeat. He did not know what would happen in respect to the organization of the House, or whether the Republicans could keep a majority sufficiently loyal and disciplined to pass the legislation the party had promised. The President had come to accept Cannon's fundamental political belief that a disciplined Republican party was unquestionably the party best fit to govern.[10]

An organized campaign against all progressives began after Aldrich promised to get some of his friends to help finance the campaign of the regulars. In nearly all insurgent areas Taft lent succor to those who favored his Administration, but his efforts to influence the selection of Republican candidates through the pressure of patronage was unsuccessful. In California, Iowa, Kansas, Michigan, New Hampshire, and Wisconsin, where Taft strongly supported regular candidates, insurgent triumphs damaged the President's prestige. The Republican primaries

9. Taft to O. T. Bannard, December 20, 1909, quoted in K. W. Hechler, *Insurgency: Personalities and Politics of the Taft Era* (New York, 1940), 216.
10. Taft to Mrs. Taft, March 19, 1910, Taft Papers; Pringle, *Taft*, I, 403.

5

and conventions settled the fate of forty incumbent regulars. Avowed progressives defeated most of the Administration congressmen, while only one progressive congressman failed to receive renomination.

These Administration defeats convinced the President that he would have to retreat or face certain defeat in the congressional elections of 1910. Taft had not yet reached the point where he agreed with Cannon that it was better to lose the election and retain a virile Republican minority in Congress than to have a nominal Republican majority made up partly of guerrillas.[11] In the summer of 1910 Taft set about mending the gaping hole torn in the Republican fence.

Taft's attempt to unify Republicans prior to the congressional elections of 1910 was a failure. This was very evident in New York, which had seemed to be a good place to heal the rift between Taft and the insurgents. In 1910 New York Republican politics consisted primarily of a battle for party primacy between Governor Charles Evans Hughes and the Old Guard machine, dominated by William Barnes, Timothy Woodruff, and William Ward. Supported by the machine, the Republican legislature had defeated many of Hughes' reform policies. Taft, Root, Hughes, Roosevelt, and most New York progressives agreed that the Old Guard leaders would have to be removed from their positions of party control if the Republicans were to carry New York in November. Taft tried to outmaneuver the Old Guard leaders, but his efforts soon came to nothing.[12]

Shortly thereafter Roosevelt ended his voluntary retirement from politics. With Hughes anxious for Roosevelt's aid, and with the encouragement of Lloyd Griscom, a Taft agent in New York, the former President announced his candidacy for the temporary chairmanship of the Republican state convention. The Old Guard reacted to Roosevelt's announcement in a way that discredited Taft publicly. The New York state executive committee met shortly after Roosevelt's declaration and nominated as temporary chairman Vice-President James S. Sherman, a good friend of the Old Guard. In explaining this selection Woodruff stated that the action of the committee had the full approval of the President.

The press reported that Sherman had, in fact, been in touch with Taft on the telephone, constantly advising him of the plans to defeat Roosevelt. It was alleged that Taft had approved of the continuance of Woodruff, Barnes, and Ward in power because they had promised the New

11. J. D. Cannon to C. D. Norton, July 21, 1910, Taft Papers.
12. T. L. Woodruff to Hilles, March 23, 1910, Hilles to Woodruff, March 25, 1910, Hilles Papers.

York state delegation to the President in 1912. Taft denied the charges. He declared that never had he heard Sherman's name suggested before the committee met. Nevertheless, columns of assertions continued to appear in the New York press which led to outbursts by Roosevelt against Taft. Roosevelt carried his fight to the convention floor, where the assembled delegates elected him as their chairman and approved his personal selection of Henry L. Stimson as the gubernatorial nominee.[13]

Thereafter the New York campaign took on national implications. To the public it appeared that Roosevelt was the leader of reform against Taft and a tainted machine. Stimson, as Roosevelt's hand-picked candidate, clearly represented progressive Republicanism as opposed to stand-pattism. A victory for Stimson would be a victory for Roosevelt and a defeat for Taft. Despite the fact that Taft genuinely admired Stimson, he admitted that "it would seem rather embarrassing if Roosevelt carried New York and I lost Ohio."[14] The campaign in New York began with Taft and the progressives against the state machine and in general agreement on the state candidates and the platform; it ended with personal bitterness between Taft and Roosevelt and a party more widely split than before.

The pre-election campaign in Ohio, like the contest in New York, had significance beyond local considerations. The whole nation looked to Ohio for a sign of dissatisfaction with the Taft Administration. The Republican chances for victory seemed slim. While the Democrats, under the popular leadership of Governor Judson Harmon, were stronger than they had been in years, antagonism between reform and conservative Republicans had damaged the Republican organization and even divided the Old Guard itself into factions.

The struggle for party control centered on the state convention and the selection of a gubernatorial candidate. Prior to the Republican convention in the summer of 1910, there was a great deal of political confusion among Old Guardsmen. George B. Cox, the boss of Cincinnati, was pushing the candidacy of O. B. Brown, a newspaperman from Zanesville. Senator Theodore E. Burton was backing away from an agreement with Cox to support Brown, and he was "praying for a case of dysentery . . . to keep him away from the convention." Former Senator Joseph B. Foraker, it was reported, "grins with delight at the

13. Taft to J. S. Sherman, August 14, 1910, to L. C. Griscom, August 20, 1910, to C. D. Norton, August 22, 23, 1910, and to Charles Taft, September 10, 1910, Taft Papers.
14. Taft to Charles Taft, October 18, 1910, Taft Papers.

confusions and says Harding is the only man he's interested in." And Senator Charles Dick kept bringing up the name of Carmi Thompson, Assistant Secretary of the Interior, for governor.[15]

Whatever plans the Old Guard forces were trying to formulate, they kept them from the press. In contact with the White House, they received Taft's agreement that he would not try to name the gubernatorial nominee. Potential nominee Warren G. Harding, a newspaperman from Marion, journeyed to Washington to receive Taft's assurance that his candidacy was not distasteful to the President. Just before the convention, he wrote to Taft reminding him of the importance of keeping out of the nominating convention and assuring the President that "both as a public speaker and an editor I have been your loyal supporter . . . solely because I believe you are right and doing a great work worthily and wisely."[16]

Progressive Republicans made open appeals for their cause. Their members in the Ohio legislature announced that they would battle to carry the party, and as the convention approached, James R. Garfield, son of President James A. Garfield, emerged as their leader. He had followed an independent political course which had aroused the enmity of Mark Hanna. Roosevelt admitted Garfield back into politics in 1902 during his anti-Hanna crusade, and in 1907 Garfield became Roosevelt's Secretary of the Interior. Disturbed by the dispute over conservation and Taft's failure to reappoint him to the Cabinet, Garfield was bitterly anti-Administration.

So strong was the conservative distaste for Garfield that the Old Guard united against his candidacy. Cox announced that his county delegation would walk out of the convention if Garfield were nominated. At the convention the contest narrowed down to three Old Guardsmen: O. B. Brown, Cox's candidate; Nicholas Longworth, congressman from Cincinnati and Burton's choice; and Warren Harding, Foraker's selection. The evening before the nominations, Cox believed he had Senator Burton's promise to swing the Cleveland delegation behind Brown. When their votes went to Longworth, Cox became very angry at what he considered a betrayal, and switched the Cincinnati votes to Harding, thereby securing his nomination. The episode left a bitter feeling between Cox and Burton.[17]

15. G. J. Karger to C. D. Norton, July 14, 1910, Hilles Papers.
16. W. G. Harding to Taft, July 16, 1910, Hilles Papers.
17. H. L. Warner, "Ohio's Crusade for Reform, 1897-1917" (Ph.D. Thesis, Harvard University, 1950), 404-5; Joseph Garretson to Taft, July 28, 1910, W. H. Ellis to Taft, July 30, 1910, Hilles Papers.

The progressives were most disappointed in the convention and in the standpat platform. Roosevelt expressed his dismay in a letter to Garfield. Taft, on the other hand, was delighted that the convention had turned Garfield down, and thought the platform was all that could be asked for. "I think Harding is proving to be as good a candidate as we could have nominated," he said.[18]

The main task after the convention was to organize the Old Guard in a concerted drive to victory. The Cox-Burton dispute erupted into the news, and a conference of Harding with the Old Guard leaders seemed essential. Backed by the President, Harding took an active part in the selection of the state chairman and the state central committee. Harding chose Lewis Laylin for the state chairman, Malcolm Jennings for the secretary of the central committee and Harry Daugherty as his campaign adviser. Laylin had been Speaker of the Ohio House and had headed the state ticket in three campaigns. Jennings was secretary of the Marion *Star*, Harding's newspaper. Daugherty was a member of the Ohio legislature who had worked hard for Harding's nomination.[19]

The selection of candidates and the choice of Harding's advisers indicated that the standpatters were in control of the Republican party in Ohio. The progressives were slow to enter the campaign, thereby adding to the impression that Harding had the support only of the Old Guard. In the final days of the campaign many friends of the Administration, including Secretaries Franklin MacVeagh and George W. Wickersham, entered Ohio to speak for the Republican candidates. If Taft did not expect a Republican victory in Ohio, he did believe that the Old Guard forces would make a good showing for the Administration.[20] But, whatever the results, it was abundantly clear that the Republican party in Ohio was sharply divided.

The congressional campaign of 1910 brought not only personal suspicion between Taft and Roosevelt; it revealed an ideological disagreement that neither had fully recognized before. After Roosevelt committed himself to campaign in New York, he set out on a tour of the West in an effort to restore party harmony. During the trip the former President introduced his program of New Nationalism which, from Taft's point of view, went quite beyond anything Roosevelt had advocated as President. Taft thought that the only feasible policies of the New Nationalism

18. Taft to Charles Taft, September 10, 1910, Taft Papers.
19. Taft to A. I. Vorys, August 7, 1910, Taft Papers; Hilles to C. D. Norton, August 12, 16, 1910, Malcolm Jennings to Hilles, August 13, 1910, A. I. Vorys to Hilles, August 5, 13, 1910, Hilles Papers.
20. Taft to A. I. Vorys, October 25, 1910, Taft Papers.

9

were those he was trying to put through. The others, he believed, were utterly impractical because they could never be obtained without a revolution or revision of the Constitution.[21]

Taft was particularly distressed that Roosevelt had "yielded to the pressure for initiative and referendum, and recall, and the direct primary—in none of which he really believes—but he thinks it wise to let the people have their head for the time being." Most disturbing, however, was Roosevelt's attack on the courts. There was throughout the insurgent West, Taft wrote to Senator Root, a bitterness against the judiciary that Roosevelt's attitude was intended to stir up. His regret that state courts had the power to set aside statutes was, Taft said, an attack on the American system at the very point where it was the strongest. "Indeed, my fear is that in this regard he simply spoke the truth as to his own views."[22]

Roosevelt's radical views, as expressed in the campaign of 1910, helped to stabilize Taft's hitherto uncertain course. Taft was bound to say that Roosevelt's speeches were more egotistic than they ever were, and that Roosevelt had allowed himself to fall into a style that made one think he considered himself still the President of the United States. It seemed as if Roosevelt deeply regretted that he had not accepted another term. Taft told one of his brothers of an allegedly authoritative report that Roosevelt was determined to become a candidate for 1912. The President noted that many of the newspapers were saying that he was about to give way and allow Roosevelt to be nominated. There was not a word of truth in it. Taft, at last, considered himself the champion of conservative interests and the thing of all others that he was not going to do was to step out of the way when Roosevelt was advocating wild ideas that contained a threat to most institutions of American stability.[23]

The election results emphasized Republican difficulties and added to the party division. The campaign of 1910 ended in an overwhelming defeat for the Republican party, particularly for regular Republicanism. In the states where the Republican party was standpat, Democrats won; in those where the party was progressive, by and large its candidates triumphed. Democrats gained a majority in the House and, while Republicans maintained control of the Senate, the progressives held the balance of power between the regulars and the Democrats. Republican defeats at the state level were also severe. Taft's fear that he would lose

21. Taft to Charles Taft, September 10, 1910, Taft Papers.
22. Taft to Elihu Root, October 15, 1910, Taft Papers.
23. Taft to Charles Taft, September 10, 16, 1910, Taft Papers.

face from an Ohio defeat and a New York Republican victory was not realized. Both New York and Ohio went overwhelmingly Democratic, with the Ohio result symptomatic of the national trend, as the Democrats won their most sweeping victory in two decades.

The election left no doubt that the Republican party was in for an enormous job of rehabilitation if it were to have any chance for success in the election of 1912. Yet the election convinced most progressive and regular Republicans that the other camp was to blame for defeat. Each side assumed that its leadership was best for the party's future. Judging from the progressive victories amidst a wave of regular defeats, the progressives reasoned that the electorate approved of their reform spirit and steadfast opposition to high tariff and anti-conservation policies. Judging from Roosevelt's setback in New York and the general Democratic sweep, regulars concluded that the voters had repudiated radicalism. The major effect of the election of 1910 was to secure the party division that had begun before 1908.

2. THE OLD GUARD
COUNTERATTACK

President Taft was a more determined and astute party leader after the debacle of the mid-term elections of 1910. Hardened by months of political frustration, he emerged confident of his own convictions and certain of his course of action. Republican division over issues, ideology, and party control convinced him that, in the long run, the nation would be served best if the Old Guard, representing a "sane" conservative view, retained its position of primacy in the Republican party. Throughout 1911 and 1912, Taft devoted himself to the fulfillment of his new political purpose, thereby avoiding most of the political bumbling so characteristic of his first eighteen months in office. Yet the press and the public remained largely unaware of any significant alterations in either presidential actions or attitudes, and it is interesting to note that historians have not recorded them. This was so because Taft's most successful maneuvers occurred outside the public spotlight, at quiet gatherings of regular leaders, or in the office of Charles Dewey Hilles, secretary to the President.

Although the exact moment of Taft's metamorphosis is unknown, it is a myth that he reacted only when La Follette and Roosevelt forced his hand. Taft seized the political initiative early in 1911, at least three months before La Follette announced his candidacy, eight months before Roosevelt privately decided to run again, and ten months before he issued a formal statement of his intentions. In April, 1911, the President began to plan for an extended tour through the heartland of insurgent territory in the West. While Taft said publicly that he wished to feel the national pulse on those issues which would be contested in November, he privately concluded that Republicanism had to maintain its conservatism and not fall heir to the progressives.[1] The proposed western tour marked the beginning of the campaign for Taft's renomination. It was decidedly political, but any attempts to influence the public mind were secondary to efforts for mobilizing the Old Guard.

The tour, which began on September 15, lasted seven weeks, with the President traveling over 13,000 miles through more than twenty states and delivering over 330 speeches, many of them brief talks from the

1. Taft to Robert Taft, August 27, 1911, and to W. M. Crane, August 30, 1911, Taft Papers.

rear of his special train. The keynote of Taft's speechmaking was his insistence that he was not to be regarded as either a standpatter or an insurgent, but that he was steering a course between the two. The reaction to his speeches served to bolster Taft's morale. The crowds were large and friendly, although estimates of their size and warmth varied with the sentiments of local newspapers. A large number of viewers, glad to interrupt their daily routines, came only to gape at the distinguished visitor in their midst, but the President was nonetheless pleased at the rapport established between himself and the people.

While the President spoke his mind at public gatherings, Hilles carried on more important political work. In the sixteen states where Taft spoke extensively, the secretary established contact with stalwart leaders, recommended measures for organizing them, and solicited opinions about the use of patronage. Usually alone, but occasionally with the President, Hilles conferred with hundreds of politicians, officeholders, and civic leaders. These political sessions were not always with supporters of the President: in California, Hilles spoke for two hours with Gavin McNab, the Democratic boss of San Francisco, who agreed to help the Taft forces in order to destroy the progressive Republicans in that city.[2] All of these efforts enabled Taft and Hilles to learn where the President was likely to have delegate support at the next national convention and where strong Old Guard action could swing the balance to Taft.

Discussions with party leaders in the West showed that Republicans were badly divided, as Hilles and the President had known, but the trip also provided the basis for considerable encouragement. Hilles felt that insurgency would be crushed in several states if the regulars mobilized. Thus, in Iowa, where the stalwarts were pilotless, Hilles appointed Taft managers, while elsewhere he gained the support of important Republican leaders. In only three states of the tour did the President appear to have little or no chance of capturing delegates, and in the very center of anti-Administration sentiment, 102 delegates seemed almost certain for the President, 116 were in doubt, while only 62 were against him.

The press, far off the mark, maintained that the President's trip had no effect on the national political situation; but the tour was most significant. It set in motion Taft's drive for conservative control of the Republican party and left him both optimistic and confident that he would be renominated. "It will be difficult for us to find any candidate but me," he wrote, "and even the Wall Street growlers will probably

2. Hilles, "Confidential Notes: September 15 to November 15, 1911," 33, 87, 78, 29, 4-5, 18, Hilles Papers.

find in my Democratic opponent—if I am nominated—a more radical man than myself; at least, one whose views are less certain in respect to the conservative principles and institutions of our Government, and therefore they will be bound to come to me anyhow."[3]

When he returned to his Washington desk early in November, the President placed the major responsibility for his renomination in Hilles' hands, and the secretary began at once a heavy schedule of work.[4] His goal was to obtain at least a majority, 540 delegates, at the next Republican convention. He surveyed the political situation state by state, continued his nationwide correspondence, and held conferences with many Taft Republicans at the White House. By the time the Republican National Committee met in Washington on December 11, Hilles knew what action to take throughout the nation.

The secretary planned to encourage Taft men in each state to take charge of the political machinery which determined the selection of convention delegates. In most cases this meant the placement of Taft men on the Republican National Committee and on the state committees. With this control, Taft men would call for state conventions early in 1912, before any other Republican candidates could gain much support. These state conventions—in some instances district conventions—would pass resolutions endorsing the program of the Administration and instructing delegates for the President. Where state law provided for presidential preference primaries, control was more difficult. It was, therefore, a corollary of Hilles' plan that almost any movement to replace convention selection of delegates by primaries should be stopped.

For two reasons the secretary was optimistic about the President's chance for renomination. First, regular Republicans controlled enough state machinery to guarantee the President a sizable block of delegates at the national convention. Second, anti-Taft sentiment was generally weak, even in the insurgent Middle West. The tour convinced Hilles that La Follette, who had announced his candidacy in June, was only popular enough to win delegates in a few scattered areas. Unless progres-

3. Taft to J. C. Hemphill, November 16, 1911, Hilles Papers.
4. Taft's selection of Hilles to manage his political fortunes not only reflected the President's confidence in his secretary, who a few years earlier had been a political unknown, but more significantly indicated Taft's sympathy with the Old Guard, for Hilles, a friend of the regulars, was a severe critic of Roosevelt. In time Hilles became the President's chief political adviser and, in July 1912, after guiding Taft's pre-convention campaign, he became Chairman of the Republican National Committee. For an account of Hilles' rise to prominence, see my article, "The Charles Dewey Hilles Papers," *The Yale University Library Gazette*, XXXVI (July, 1961), 1-12.

sive and other dissatisfied Republicans found a more forceful figure to lead their insurgency, Hilles was sure that most delegates would support the President. There was considerable talk of Roosevelt for President; admittedly he would be a formidable opponent. But Roosevelt had not announced his candidacy, and many of his friends doubted that he would. Even that threat, if it actually came, could be foiled by the early acquisition of a large number of delegates.

From the vantage point of December, 1911, the President appeared to be in good position to gain victory on the first convention ballot. Although none of the delegates could be chosen legally until after the Republican National Committee issued a call for their selection, Taft men had already prepared the way for the control of 404 of the 1,078 delegates. Another 304 were doubtful, but within the reach of Taft men. Only 370 potential delegate votes appeared to be in control of anti-Taft forces, and of these Hilles conceded just 72 as absolutely against the President. This encouraging view, based on the best reports available, was predicated on the supposition that La Follette rather than Roosevelt would be Taft's prime opponent.

The core of delegate strength for the President came from those areas where the party machinery was safely in the hands of regular forces—in the territories and Washington, D. C., controlled by Republican federal officeholders; in Arkansas, Florida, and Mississippi, where the Republican organizations were without some kind of internal dissension; and in seven small states such as Rhode Island, where there were no primaries and where one party leader wielded great influence. Additionally, the skill of individual leadership brought a few large state organizations, such as those of New York and Indiana, into the Taft fold before the end of 1911, despite strong antagonism to the Old Guard.

The greatest prize at the convention, New York's 90 votes, was secured by the forcefulness of William Barnes, who became chairman of the New York state committee early in 1911. An old line conservative, Barnes had lost power during the attempt in 1910 to free the party from Old Guard domination, but the Democratic gubernatorial victory enabled him to regain party influence. Henry L. Stimson and Herbert Parsons, among Taft's more progressive advocates in New York, complained against placing the party in the hands of a reactionary like Barnes. However, his organizational ability and his devotion to the President were strong recommendations for White House support of Barnes' leadership. During the summer and fall of 1911, Barnes worked closely with such old-time party leaders as William L. Ward, Timothy

15

Woodruff, and Vice-President Sherman in perfecting a strong state organization. Republican recapture of the state assembly in the November elections of 1911 so strengthened the hand of this Old Guard contingent that, by the end of the year, Barnes was sure he could deliver the New York delegation.[5]

Indiana support for Taft represented a triumph for the Old Guard over factional conflict and over subservience to the progressive organization of Senator Beveridge. After the Senator's defeat for re-election in 1910, the Old Guard successfully compromised most of its internal differences. The President and Hilles aided this unification by acquiescing to the requests of the faction led by retiring Committeeman Harry S. New, who was in a struggle with State Chairman Edwin M. Lee for Old Guard domination. In return for promises of presidential support, Taft dispensed Indiana patronage at the suggestion of New. With defeat apparent, Lee gave up his struggle and withdrew as state chairman in the hope of salvaging at least a federal appointment for himself, but the President, at New's insistence, denied Lee any position. By the end of the year, it was clear that the united Old Guard of Indiana would be able to wrest party control from the Beveridge organization at the state party conference in January, and that they could secure most of the state's delegation for the President.[6]

If the President expected to win renomination on the first ballot, he had to hold all 404 delegates favoring him and acquire at least another 136. What stood in his path were factional disputes within Old Guard state organizations, contests for personal power among southern Republicans, a tradition of progressivism in the party, personal antagonism to Taft, and several presidential primary contests. Until most of these obstacles were overcome and regular Republicans achieved unity, as they had in Indiana, the President's chances remained in doubt.

Typical of the serious nature of Old Guard factionalism were conditions in Oklahoma, where two irreconcilable groups, both favoring the President, were vying for leadership. One clique consisted of the men who had supported Taft for the nomination in 1908: State Chairman James A. Harris and Congressmen Bird McGuire and Dick Morgan.

5. William Barnes to Taft, January 23, 1911, Hilles to Taft(?), May 13, 1911, Taft Papers; Herbert Parsons to Hilles, June 19, 1911, W. L. Ward to Hilles, July 17, 1911, T. L. Woodruff to Taft, July 18, 1911, unknown correspondent to Hilles, July 26, 1911, William Barnes to Hilles, September 15, November 14, December 21, 1911, Hilles Papers.

6. Hilles, "Confidential Notes," 31-32, Taft to J. C. Hemphill, November 16, 1911, Hilles Papers.

National Committeeman Cash Cade and his aide, Dennis T. Flynn, leaders of the other crowd, had angered the Harris faction by distributing practically all of the federal patronage in the state. Both groups promised to work for a Taft delegation, but each wanted the President's support. Yet intervention could be dangerous. If the conflict for supremacy drew the Administration to one side, the other might oppose the President's renomination.[7]

Obstacles to gaining delegates for the President arose, too, in southern states where the Republican party was without hope of election victory. These southern organizations, creatures of the Republican Administration, were kept alive on a diet of federal patronage in order to secure favorable delegates at national conventions. The key southern Republicans were the referees, usually the national committeemen, who had the dual responsibility of recommending federal appointees and keeping them in line at convention time. But in 1911 new leaders challenged the positions of several referees. North Carolina posed the most difficult situation because of the bitter feud between National Committeeman E. C. Duncan and former Congressman John M. Morehead, each of whom had the support of Republicans professing loyalty to the President's cause.[8] Division in South Carolina and Georgia concerned not only the power to recommend the distribution of federal patronage, but the question of the role of the Negro in the party. Younger white men, assisted by Negroes who felt that colored people were being denied party representation, disputed the long-time leadership of Committeeman John G. Capers of South Carolina and former Committeeman Clark Grier of Georgia.[9] Charges of selfishness and disloyalty by one group had to be weighed against similar countercharges from other groups. Before northern insurgent activity could complicate the southern political scene, Hilles had to put the weight of the Administration behind the factions which had the influence to call pro-Taft conventions.

7. Hilles, "Confidential Notes," 74-76, Bird McGuire to Hilles, July 27, 1911, and to Taft, August 6, November 15, 1911, D. T. Morgan to Hilles, August 23, 1911, D. T. Flynn to Hilles, December 15, 1911, Hilles Papers.

8. J. M. Morehead to Taft, January 30, 1911, and to Hilles November 24, December 20, 1911, G. J. Karger to C. D. Norton, February 7, 1911, Marion Butler to Hilles, July 6, 1911, Thomas Settle to W. M. Crane, November 26, 1911, and to Hilles, November 27, December 14, 1911, Hilles Papers.

9. J. G. Capers to Hilles, April 18, May 9, 1911, T. L. Grant to Hilles, July 26, 1911, L. W. C. Blaylock to Hilles, October 9, 1911, Clark Grier to Hilles, May 22, July 3, 11, 1911, H. S. Jackson to Hilles, May 2, 31, July 11, 21, September 20, November 2, 16, 1911, and to J. H. Hammond, November 29, 1911, W. H. Johnson to Hilles, July 26, August 8, December 19, 1911, D. B. Atherton to Hilles, June 1, 1911, Hilles Papers.

One of Hilles' major decisions was to carry the preconvention fight everywhere, including the most anti-Administration states. Even if this resulted in failure to capture a single delegate, the effort would keep insurgents busy in their own backyards, and there was always the chance of capturing a few, if not a majority, of the 370 anti-Taft delegates. Any regular victory in insurgent territory would have an encouraging effect on Taft men everywhere. Considering the vicissitudes of politics, the best plans might go astray, and although Hilles anticipated losing some apparently secure delegates he hoped to compensate with gains in insurgent areas. Perhaps the best Administration possibilities lay in the capture of the anti-Taft organizations of those states which had no primaries. Any success in these areas, however, faced two major hurdles: the personal antagonism to the President of influential party leaders and the popularity of La Follette and Roosevelt.

The support of the Texas delegation, for example, depended on Committeeman Cecil Lyon, a warm friend of Theodore Roosevelt. Reports reached Hilles that Lyon was holding the threat of patronage over the heads of federal officeholders in an effort to prevent the selection of a Taft delegation. Apparently he planned to take an uncommitted group to the convention with the hope of throwing its support to Roosevelt. Unless the Taft men of Texas took quick action, the 40 delegates of that state would slip away by default.[10]

Senator Albert Cummins was the great stumbling block in Iowa. A favorite son candidate who was markedly popular in his own state, Cummins wanted to use the Iowa delegation as a force at the conventions for some progressive, if not for himself. Friendly Administration congressmen told Hilles that Senator Cummins was engineering a party realignment which he was going to use to force Senator William S. Kenyon into his camp. With proper leadership, however, Kenyon would not bow to the pressure. Acting on the advice of former Senator Lafayette Young, Hilles appointed John T. Adams as head of the President's pre-convention affairs. Adams had managed the last campaign for Senator Allison and, according to George Roberts of the Treasury Department, he was the best man in Iowa for the task.[11] At the very least, Hilles hoped to keep Cummins engaged in Iowa.

10. S. A. Hackworth to Taft, February 28, 1911, W. B. Brush to C. D. Norton, March 7, 1911, R. H. Bruce to Hilles, August 7, 1911, P. H. Stretton to Hilles, January 30, 1912, Hilles Papers.
11. Hilles, "Confidential Notes," 33-34, G. E. Roberts to Franklin MacVeagh, October 13, 1911, F. A. Nimocks to unknown recipient, October 23, 1911, Hilles Papers.

Illinois presented the dual problem of a very active La Follette campaign and a disunited Old Guard. La Follette's promoters considered Illinois one of the most favorable battlegrounds for his campaign. Even before their man's formal announcement, La Follette's men organized with vigor, persistence, and apparently an unlimited amount of funds. In November La Follette opened his midwestern headquarters in Chicago, while his followers entered into strenuous activity on his behalf. Meanwhile, the regulars remained divided by personal animosities and the conflicting ambitions of Governor Charles S. Deneen, Senator Shelby M. Cullom, former Senator William Lorimer and former Governor Richard Yates. The federal officials, including Len Small, Assistant Treasurer of the United States, Dan Campbell, Postmaster of Chicago, and Frank Smith, an internal revenue agent at Chicago, were not working in harmony. A forceful guiding hand was needed to unite the regulars if they were to overcome the advantage of La Follette. Speaker Cannon and Congressman William B. McKinley, perhaps the two best organizers in the state, could not be used. Cannon had too many enemies within the party, while McKinley was engaged as chairman of the Republican Congressional Campaign Committee. One of Hilles' major difficulties in the coming year was to be the selection of a Taft leader in Illinois.[12]

In California, where anti-Taft leaders controlled the political machinery, Administration prospects looked very dim. The insurgents had taken command of the Republican party when they gained control of the state convention in 1910 and nominated Hiram Johnson for governor. Shortly afterwards, the insurgents, who dominated the state legislature, recast the election laws of the state, but they carefully left a paragraph which had been inserted in the laws in 1908 when the stalwarts were supreme. The effect of that paragraph was to give a tenure of two years to a delegate elected to county or state conventions. Thus those delegates who attended state and county conventions in the summer of 1910 would not be superseded until the summer of 1912. They would meet in their several congressional districts and in their state convention in the spring of 1912 to select delegates to the national convention. Since the delegates in 1912 would be almost the same as·those who voted for Johnson in 1910, it was generally understood that the governor and his associates could select their own nominee. The John-

12. Hilles to Taft, May 28, 1911, L. H. Miner to Taft, May 11, 1911, F. O. Lowden to Taft, July 7, 1911, G. J. Karger to Hilles, September 11, 1911, G. S. Wood to Hilles, November 2, 1911, Hilles Papers.

son crowd favored La Follette, although they were willing to support Roosevelt if he declared himself a candidate, but they were unalterably opposed to Taft's renomination. Taft's supporters were, therefore, disheartened and demoralized. As Hilles reported to the President, they were the old cavalry guard which had been unhorsed and had no compelling captain. They felt that no power on earth could prevent the state from sending a La Follette or Roosevelt delegation to the national convention.[13]

One hope for the regulars remained. California had adopted a woman's suffrage amendment in the fall of 1911. This broadening of the electorate provided an excellent excuse for the friends of the President to start an agitation for a presidential preference primary. Otherwise, they argued, the 380,000 women voters of California would not have a choice at selection of a candidate for the presidency until 1916. Regulars hoped that the women would complain that they were being denied complete and immediate franchisement, and that this pressure would compel Governor Johnson to recommend that the legislature cure this defect in existing election laws. While on the western tour, Hilles casually suggested to Meyer Lissner, the insurgent state chairman, that Taft men would be satisfied to have the Republicans of California express their individual preferences for President. One of the ten commandments of the progressives, Hilles reminded Lissner, was "Thou shall not maintain ring rule." But Lissner replied that, while a primary sounded good in theory, he had not been persuaded that it would work well in practice. He added that he would wait until some of the older states, such as Ohio, had made the experiment.[14] Therefore, the Old Guard expected to present itself as the champion of the presidential primary, while at the same time they branded the insurgents as the enemies of this progressive measure. Certainly this example of practical politics was an Alice in Wonderland spectacle.

Any successful Taft movement in California needed organization, but the Old Guard leaders were generally disorganized and discredited with the voters. Former Senator Frank Flint was the bête noire in Southern California and M. H. DeYoung, owner of the San Francisco *Chronicle*, was the whipping boy for insurgents in the northern part of the state.

13. Hilles, "Confidential Notes," 5-7, J. R. Knowland to Taft, October 22, November 1, 1910, G. J. Karger to Hilles May 10, 1911, C. M. Hammond to Taft, July 9, August 11, 1911, W. M. Chadbourne to Hilles, September 18, 28, 1911, Hilles Papers.

14. Hilles, "Confidential Notes," 11-12, 20, Hilles Papers; Taft to Horace Taft, November 5, 1911, Taft Papers.

20

Congressmen Julius Kahn and Joseph R. Knowland and Senator George C. Perkins had too many enemies among the regulars to take charge of Taft's affairs. Someone had to be found who had not been prominently identified with factional fights and who could effectively lead a group of respected but politically inexperienced businessmen in a state-wide club for the President. Late in December Senator Perkins recommended Charles Mifflin Hammond as the perfect man to head the Taft Committee of California. Hammond had been a devoted friend of Perkins, a Roosevelt-Fairbanks elector, and chairman of the Lake County Republican committee for twelve years. He was generally unknown throughout the state, and his greatest claim to fame was that he was Theodore Roosevelt's brother-in-law.[15] While the President's chances for success in California were slim, a Taft movement was set in motion before the end of 1911.

Even though the progressive tradition was strong in states which selected their delegates by primary vote, such as Wisconsin and the Dakotas, Hilles attempted, however feebly, to organize Taft forces and to place a full slate of Administration delegates on the primary ballots. In Oregon and Ohio action for Taft was better than perfunctory.

The Oregon primary law placed a premium on party maneuvering by providing that each elector vote for only one convention delegate. Since the ten men who received the largest number of votes became the Oregon delegates, the important factor was not the total strength of the Taft forces but rather the way in which votes were distributed for Taft delegates. "Capable organization," Hilles said, "will distribute the strength to a nicety; lack of organization may result in a wasteful bunching of the hits."[16] With the assistance of Committeeman Ralph E. Williams, Congressman W. C. Hawley, and the Portland collector of internal reve-

15. Hammond used his connection with the Roosevelt family and his disapproval of Roosevelt's progressivism for his political advancement. He wrote to Taft, for example: "Roosevelt was out here in March. The Harvard Club of San Francisco gave him a dinner. I was present and heard his speech. After dinner I went up to him and said: 'Theodore (he is my brother-in-law), that was a good speech, but I do not agree with you on any of your new-fangled ideas.' He looked at me as though I was crazy, and then asked me if I was not solid for Hiram Johnson. At which I blew up, and the standers by said afterwards that my language was not fit for publication." C. M. Hammond to Taft July 9, 1911, Hilles Papers. Actually Hammond's relationship with Roosevelt was very tenuous. Hammond's wife and Theodore Roosevelt's first wife were sisters. Hammond did not marry until four years after Roosevelt's first wife died. See also Hilles, "Confidential Notes," 9-12, J. R. Knowland to Hilles, October 5, 1911, G. C. Perkins to C. M. Hammond, December 27, 1911, Hilles Papers.

16. Hilles, "Confidential Notes," 77-85, Hilles Papers.

nue, David M. Dunne, Hilles put together a committee of representative and resourceful Republicans which received official sanction from the President. The committee consisted of eighteen men who had been financially active for Taft in 1908, and who had signified their willingness to volunteer in a Taft movement. The group, designed as a directing agency in the coming presidential fight, was empowered to form auxiliary committees in every county. Despite the opposition of Jonathan Bourne, one of the President's leading enemies in the United States Senate, and the reform tradition in Oregon, Taft's friends thought the President had a fair chance to capture the April primary.[17]

In his home state of Ohio, Taft's candidacy faced strong progressive opposition as well as a primary contest. The militant reformers, having achieved a partial triumph by reframing the state laws, were determined to complete the task by driving out the Old Guard and remolding the party organization to reflect the spirit of the times. The progressives might conceivably have toned down their demands if they could have cooperated with the regulars, but no move could be made without considering its effect on Taft's candidacy, and the Old Guard frequently found it impossible to compromise with the anti-Taft, progressive wing.

The President and Hilles cooperated with the conservative faction which dominated the Republican state committee. Arthur I. Vorys, Hilles' long-time friend, acted as coordinator of the Taft movement, and his right-hand man was Lewis C. Laylin, Republican state chairman in 1910, formerly Speaker of the Ohio House and Secretary of State. Two of their most active agents were Malcolm Jennings and Harry M. Daugherty. Jennings was the secretary of the executive committee and Warren G. Harding's business partner; Daugherty was a political friend of both, who pledged his utmost strength for the Taft cause. The President also enjoyed the favor of the men who had led the Republican party for the past half-dozen years: Senator Burton, former Senator Dick, Harding, and Rudolph Hynicka, George B. Cox's successor in Cincinnati. Federal appointees, such as Maurice Maschke in Cleveland, kept city organizations loyal.

During the fall of 1911, anti-Taft activity increased in intensity. The first to organize against the Old Guard were the progressives in the Cleveland area, the main center of discontent. The Ohio Progressive

17. W. C. Hawley to Hilles, August 16, September 1, 1911, D. M. Dunne to Hilles, October 3, 1911, E. B. Piper to Hilles, October 27, 1911, J. W. Hill to Hilles, November 6, 1911, Ben Selling to Hilles, November 17, December 2, 1911, Hilles Papers.

Republican League, formed in Cleveland on November 3, soon expanded into twenty-four counties. Initially La Follette had the advantage because he was the avowed candidate, but at a dinner on November 20, the Roosevelt contingent, led by James R. Garfield, presented the former President's name as the next nominee. Roosevelt, while privately stating that such an endorsement made him uncomfortable, did nothing to stop it. A number of newspapers declared for Roosevelt shortly thereafter.[18]

At this time Walter F. Brown, chairman of the Republican state central committee, apparently convinced that his political future could best be served outside the Taft camp, publicly announced his preference for Roosevelt. Brown's tactics became clear when he sent out letters to various members of the state central committee. His intention was to change the primary so that it would include, in addition to the 42 congressional district delegates, the 6 delegates-at-large normally chosen at a state convention.[19]

In order to block Brown's primary proposal, the Old Guard leaders maneuvered to retain control of the state central committee. Following the orders of Vorys and Laylin, who felt that the Taft organization could counteract progressive influence most effectively at the state level, the regulars held in abeyance political activity in the congressional districts. Various stalwarts, unaware of the reason for the lack of local activity, complained that nothing was being done to stop the progressives. Hilles and the President knew, however, that a sufficient organization existed to meet the most immediate threat to the Taft campaign in Ohio.[20]

The meeting of the Republican National Committee in Washington on December 11 brought the Taft campaign of 1911 to a climax. Under

18. Warner, "Ohio's Crusade," 572-80; Hilles, "Confidential Notes," 72-73, Malcolm Jennings to Hilles, August 1, 1911, Hilles Papers; Taft to J. C. Hemphill, November 16, 1911, Taft Papers.

19. Brown's circular letter read: "Reports that come to me from all over the state indicate that the political situation is becoming critical. Republicans generally seem to be looking forward to next year with little hope or interest. . . .

"Whatever may be our individual notions as to who the Republican nominee for the presidency should or should not be, it does not seem the part of wisdom to let the impression go abroad that the party organization contemplates running a roadroller over the opposition to Taft. Should we not in some manner arrange to submit the issue to the Republicans of the state?

"Please advise me whether you favor calling a meeting of the State Central Committee in the course of a week or two, to exchange views and to try to find some method of clarifying the situation." W. F. Brown to G. H. Hamilton, November 17, 1911, Hilles Papers.

20. Malcolm Jennings to Hilles, November 25, 1911, G. J. Karger to Hilles, December 5, 1911, W. Y. H. Black to Taft, December 11, 1911, A. I. Vorys to Hilles, December 23, 1911, Hilles Papers.

strong pressure from Hilles, the committee completed its business in one day, resolving all measures to the advantage of the President. In quick order the committee voted down a proposal to institute nation-wide primaries and a plan to reduce southern delegate strength. Additionally, the committee appointed an entirely pro-Taft subcommittee on arrangements for the convention. Harry S. New of Indiana retained the chairmanship, and four other staunch Taft supporters—Arthur I. Vorys of Ohio, David W. Mulvane of Kansas, Franklin Murphy of New Jersey, and Ralph E. Williams of Oregon—joined him on the subcommittee. Since this body played an important part in selecting the keynote speaker and the temporary and permanent chairmen, the President was almost assured of favorable decisions from the convention rostrum. The committee completed its work by designating Chicago as the convention site and setting June 18 as the day of the first session.

The national committee meeting had been an unqualified success for the President. It helped to guarantee that the pre-convention fight would follow the customary course of a President seeking a second term, through patronage and through officeholders who also would be delegates. An editorial in the New York *Tribune* reflected the sentiments of many Taft adherents when it said that the Republican National Committee meeting was harmoniously transacted. "Mr. Taft's friends were in complete control, a situation which foreshadowed what is practically certain to happen at the Republican convention." The President would be renominated because the anti-Taft movement had no candidate. La Follette was a "parochial figure," whose name was hardly mentioned in Washington, and the only threat was the possibility of Roosevelt's candidacy. Such talk, the editorial said, sprang mostly from Democratic sources, which were using Roosevelt's name only to propagate the idea of dissension and to foment enmities in the Republican party. Actually, the Roosevelt candidacy was a myth. "Before believing it," the editorial said, "we shall have to see some evidence that his political judgment has deserted him."[21]

The *Tribune* predicted badly. In February, 1912, Roosevelt formally entered the presidential campaign. When Taft heard of Roosevelt's decision, he wrote to his brother Horace, "I am not very happy these days because I don't like the character of the contest." He hated to be at odds with Theodore Roosevelt, who had made him President of the United States and towards whom he should always feel a heavy debt of gratitude on that account. "But, of course," Taft said, "he made me Presi-

21. New York *Tribune*, December 13, 1911.

dent and not deputy, and I have to be President." Roosevelt, he wrote, was "ill advised by sycophants and neurotics who feed his vanity and influence his judgment, that his usual good political sense is at fault in respect of the election. I don't know that it is in respect of the nomination, for we shall have a hard fight for that in my judgment."[22]

As Taft had feared, Roosevelt's entry into the campaign affected his cause adversely. Even before Roosevelt announced his intentions, Taft lost support in several states. In January Taft men reported that Roosevelt enthusiasts were active throughout the country, and by February many regulars admitted that the President faced a serious political test.

The primary unexpectedly became a major issue in Illinois, largely because of the Roosevelt drive in that state. Hilles conferred with Illinois federal officeholders throughout January in an effort to unite the regular forces, but at the end of the month he admitted to the President his disappointment that the Republican leaders "should sit idle and see the situation fall to pieces."[23] The campaign for delegates started without the aid of the Old Guard on February 9, when the Taft Club of Illinois organized. David R. Forgan, a Chicago banker, became president, and Julius Rosenwald, a wealthy financier, supplied much of the capital. Later that month Chauncey Dewey, the Roosevelt leader, wrote an open letter to Forgan in which he asked the Taft Club to join with the Roosevelt committee in support of a primary. Dewey proposed that the two organizations should apply to Governor Deneen, asking him to recommend a presidential preference primary to a special session of the legislature. Since Forgan believed that no primary law could be passed in time to effect the 1912 election, he thought that Dewey's proposal was an insincere display intended to discredit the Taft organization. He decided "to call Dewey's bluff," not by cooperating with him, but by being the first to request primary legislation.[24] Perhaps experienced politicians would have foreseen the danger in this maneuver, but Forgan did not. Events soon proved that Forgan had miscalculated the popularity of the primary movement in Illinois.

Progressive sentiment fed on division in the regular ranks in Oklahoma. The Roosevelt movement assumed serious proportions shortly after the fourth district instructed two delegates for Taft. The conven-

22. Taft to Horace Taft, February 15, 1912, Taft Papers. The story of Roosevelt's decision to seek election is told in Mowry, *Roosevelt and the Progressive Movement*, 189-200. Not until December, 1911, did Roosevelt turn against Taft's candidacy.
23. Hilles to Taft, January 31, 1912, Hilles Papers.
24. D. R. Forgan to Hilles, February 29, 1912, Hilles Papers.

tion, held on January 23, attracted nation-wide attention because it was the first in the country. The Roosevelt supporters packed their friends into the galleries at the opera house in Coalgate, site of the convention, in an effort to influence the decision on the floor. Fist fights and brawls frequently interrupted the noisy session. Although the Taft leaders managed to control the choice of the two delegates, the Coalgate convention revealed that Taft supporters were irreconcilably divided. Many Taft men condemned state chairman James A. Harris for injecting his candidacy as committeeman into the deliberations. Harris' enemies insisted that the state chairman had unnecessarily involved Taft in a state affair, and they said that the President would be defeated at the remaining conventions on Harris' account. Early in February George C. Priestley, a wealthy oil man and a Roosevelt booster, entered the race for committeeman against Harris. He pledged to carry his campaign into every district and thereby test the relative popularity of Taft and Roosevelt. Priestley's announcement lent strength and money to the Roosevelt managers. About the same time Cash Cade, Harris' most severe critic and the retiring national committeeman, withdrew from active participation in the pre-convention campaign. Harris, therefore, had to face the state and district conventions, scheduled in March, without the aid of a powerful wing of the Old Guard. On February 26 Harris telegraphed Hilles: "Roosevelt supporters hilarious since his announcement; sentiment growing rapidly."[25]

The Roosevelt movement also crushed the President's slim chances in California. When the California legislature passed a presidential primary on December 24, Taft men believed that the President might achieve victory in a contest with La Follette. However, the Taft organization split when the progressives abandoned La Follette early in 1912 in favor of Roosevelt. A group of the President's supporters in San Francisco, led by Charles W. Hornick, general manager of the San Francisco *Call*, announced their opposition to the Taft organization headed by Charles Mifflin Hammond. Calling themselves Progressives for Taft, the group argued that Hammond represented the old Republican machine. While professing loyalty to the President, they refused to cooperate with Hammond.[26] This division eliminated the possibility of

25. J. A. Harris to Hilles, January 23, 24, February 2, 26, 1912, J. D. Flynn to Hilles, January 28, 1912, Eugene Lorton to Hilles, January 31, 1912, C. W. Raymond to Hilles, February 17, 1912, Hilles Papers.

26. Marshall Hale and A. L. Shinn to Taft, February 29, 1912, C. W. Hornick to I. E. Bennett, February 29, 1912, Hilles Papers.

success in San Francisco, the one area in California where Taft had general popular support.

While these reports were disheartening, they did not change Hilles' view that Taft would be renominated. The Roosevelt movement seemed most effective only in those states where anti-Taft sentiment had been particularly intense before 1912. Several regular organizations even appeared to gather impetus in the face of the Roosevelt opposition. Lewis Laylin reported from Ohio, for example, that, except for Walter F. Brown and James A. Garfield, he had control of the state central committee. Laylin also said that the 6 delegates-at-large would not be elected at a primary. Vorys commented that Laylin was doing well and should not be disturbed. The idea, he said, was to promote the Taft movement wherever possible through the regular organization. He thought each committeeman would handle affairs in the various districts and that Taft would capture most of the May primaries.[27] Charles P. Taft, the President's brother, aided Laylin and Vorys with large financial contributions. "If Roosevelt is nominated on his Columbus platform for the Republican party," he said, "I shall turn democrat and that is saying a good deal."[28]

Just as Vorys worked quietly in Ohio, so did John T. Adams manage the Taft campaign against Senator Cummins in Iowa without publicity. Late in January Adams received $5,000 from the national fund to organize the regulars throughout the state. Aided by Postmaster Frank Nimocks, he prepared to control the state convention without an announced headquarters. He secretly corresponded and met with many district chairmen and received their support. Early in February Adams wrote to Hilles, "It is just beginning to dawn upon the Senator's friends that they have a fight on their hands. No one has any idea that we can control the state convention, except possibly Nimocks . . . but we are going right after it just as if we had a chance." Later the same month Adams predicted that Taft would carry the state convention. "My chief concern at the present time," he said, "is that Senator Cummins may withdraw and spoil our fun before we put on the finishing touches."[29]

Many of the regular state organizations that favored Taft in 1911 held firm against progressive opposition. Taft's expectation of capturing the 90-vote New York delegation, for example, took a long stride for-

27. A. I. Vorys to Hilles, January 19, February 1, 1912, L. C. Laylin to Hilles, January 16, 18, 23, 26, 1912, Hilles Papers.
28. Charles Taft to Hilles, February 26, 1912, Hilles Papers.
29. J. T. Adams to Hilles, January 25, 27, February 2, 19, 1912, Hilles Papers.

ward before the end of February. The key to success rested with the Republican committees in each district, since New York law provided for the primary election of delegates only after they had been selected by the district committees. While the New York primary eliminated the convention method, it did not allow for a popularity contest between Taft and Roosevelt. Under the leadership of Committeeman William Barnes, the Old Guard gained control of a majority of the district committees. During the first week in February, 23 of New York's 45 district committees pledged their support to the President, and at the month's end Taft seemed likely to secure 80 delegates for the March primaries.[30]

Perhaps most of Hilles' optimism stemmed from success in the struggle for the 278 southern delegates. Both organizations waged an exceedingly active southern canvass during the first two months of 1912, but it became clear at the end of February that the President would win nearly all of these delegates.

The initial policy of the Roosevelt forces was to send agents throughout the South to lure the officeholding group away from the Administration by one means or another. Ormsby McHarg, an experienced political organizer who had secured southern delegates for Taft in 1908, headed the Roosevelt drive. He turned against the Administration after his removal from a position as council for two Indian tribes because of his obvious uselessness to the Indians. McHarg's methods proved ineffective at the very first southern convention, which was held in Florida on February 6. The Taft leaders maintained control over officeholders, settled all contests in their favor, and chose 12 delegates pledged for the President.[31]

When McHarg realized his inability to compete for delegates in direct contest with the Administration, he changed his tactics and decided to oppose the President by fomenting party bolts. He resolved to place a Roosevelt slate of delegates in most southern states, not with the hope of winning, but in order to engineer the secession and election of contesting delegates. His aim was to bring these contests before the national committee when it made up the role of the convention in June. McHarg's decision to contest the results of most southern conventions, irrespective of their merits, was to cast suspicion on the sincerity of later contests in the North and harm Roosevelt's case before the national committee.

30. J. S. Sherman to Hilles, January 24, 1912, S. S. Koenig to Taft, January 29, 1912, W. M. Calder and M. J. Dady to Taft, January 30, 1912, Hilles to H. S. Chubb, February 2, 1912, and to Taft, February 27, 1912, Hilles Papers.
31. Mowry, *Roosevelt and the Progressive Movement*, 200; H. S. Chubb to Hilles, February 6, 7, 8, 13, 1912, Hilles Papers.

Taft men in the South met McHarg's challenge successfully, primarily because Hilles guided them skillfully. The secretary's awareness of southern politics and his personal contact with Taft men was largely responsible for a well-disciplined organization. With the secretary's support, southern leaders applied pressure on postmasters and federal officials, bluntly telling many that if they failed to support Taft at state and district conventions, they would not be reappointed. Hilles' strategy was to establish control over southern political machinery before the Roosevelt men could organize and make an impression on the country. In January Hilles wrote to each southern chairman, asking that his state and district conventions be held as early in 1912 as possible. Eight of the twelve southern committees thus called their conventions in February and March, while two others called theirs in early April. In contrast only four non-southern states held conventions before the first week in April.

One of the secretary's most difficult tasks was in Texas, where Cecil A. Lyon, the referee, was a Roosevelt enthusiast. In January Lyon announced that he would introduce a resolution at the meeting of the state executive committee to provide for the election of delegates at a general primary. Texas supporters of the President advised Hilles that Taft would lose the delegation if Hilles did not act soon to remove Lyon and the pro-Roosevelt crowd from control. Early in February Hilles called to Washington H. F. MacGregor, a Houston businessman and opponent of Lyon. The secretary placed him in charge of the state campaign and sent Joseph Kealing of Indiana to Texas as his assistant.

While the issue in Texas remained in doubt at the end of February, it appeared that Hilles had acted in time to secure the 40-vote delegation. When MacGregor returned to Texas, Lyon began to wage a campaign against him for leadership in the state. Lyon sent out a circular letter to all federal officials in which he appealed for support at the state executive committee meeting on the basis of his power as referee. The President became particularly impatient with Lyon, whose attitude, he said, was that of a man with independent power. With Administration support behind him, MacGregor predicted his control of the executive committee at its meeting in March.[32]

Throughout the South Hilles threw the weight of the Administration behind the men he believed best able to serve the President. In Georgia

32. New York *Tribune*, February 10, 27, 1912; Taft to Colonel Simpson, February 21, 1912, Taft Papers; H. F. MacGregor to Hilles, January 2, February 5, 9, 17, 20, 29, 1912, C. W. Raymond to Hilles, January 15, 1912, W. B. Brush to A. I. Vorys, January 28, 1912, Hilles Papers.

and South Carolina the secretary supported the Black and Tans against the Lily Whites. His swift recognition of pro-Taft elements was largely responsible for the inability of the Roosevelt movement to advance in Alabama, Virginia, and Tennessee. In fact, the only instance where Taft men failed to strengthen their position by the end of February was in North Carolina, where Hilles was unable to settle the dispute for leadership between former Congressman Morehead and Committeeman Duncan.

This direction of the southern political machinery paid dividends at the conventions held in February. The Roosevelt supporters failed to elect a single delegate, although they contested most of the conventions. At the district convention in Birmingham, Alabama, for example, the defeated Roosevelt men withdrew and elected their own delegates. By the end of February, 50 southern delegates pledged their support to the President, and the Administration seemed certain to gain another 160 before the middle of April.

Within a few months then, Hilles, fully supported by the President, had mobilized the disorganized Taft men into a cohesive force. Following a strategy calculated to make the best possible use of an early offensive, he relied primarily on existing Old Guard state organizations and the influence of the national Administration. Most significantly, he gained the initial political advantage by acquiring enough pledged support for Taft to withstand a later progressive drive.

Hilles' generalship was expert, his methods flexible. The secretary first secured the cooperation of Old Guardsmen who controlled party affairs in their own states and districts. Using federal agents and the pressure of patronage, he then influenced the early selection of southern delegates. His third basic maneuver was to establish or to give support to just one Taft organization in every state, even where the progressives seemed to be in command. In this way, he expected the President to overcome, at least in part, the debilitating impact of Old Guard factionalism, of apathy among regulars, and of insurgency. Finally, Hilles opposed attempts to change the traditional nominating machinery. Where it was to the President's advantage, Hilles fought against the introduction of state primaries. The secretary retained as well the support of the Republican National Committee and thereby kept intact the advantages of the convention system and southern delegate representation. He also secured control of the arrangements for the Republican national convention.

From the evidence which Hilles had at the end of February, Taft appeared to be a first ballot winner at the convention, notwithstanding the intensity of the Roosevelt movement and its success in several areas of the nation. Although efforts to unite Old Guardsmen were by no means entirely successful, Taft men controlled 24 state organizations, whose combined delegate strength was 566 delegates—26 more than the majority necessary for the nomination. While the President was likely to lose some of the 566 delegates before the convention, he also appeared in a good position to gain at least an equal number of votes from other areas, such as Texas and Iowa. Since the vagaries of politics and the dynamic appeal of the Roosevelt movement could prevent Taft's renomination, the President and Hilles anticipated a tense political struggle in the remaining three and a half months before the national convention. But they knew they had the advantage and that their forces were ready to meet all opposition through any legal means.

3. CONSERVATIVES AND PROGRESSIVES: A STUDY OF DIFFERENTIATIONS

With Taft and Roosevelt openly vying for party leadership, Republicans had at last to express a clear choice of allegiance. The decision for some was simply a matter of pursuing vested political interests, yet the ultimate stand of most Republicans was not predicated on political expediency. Regulars and progressives believed, by and large, that they were irreconcilably different. This conviction developed primarily from conflicting political ideologies rather than from any basic differences in the social and economic background of Republicans.

A significant feature of recent American historiography has been its concern with social background as a vital force in political life. Historians of the Progressive Era have devoted particular attention to this matter, and their investigations have led to the thesis, widely accepted in historical circles, that the political activity of the Progressives was largely the result of a status revolution. This position has been advanced most forcefully by Richard Hofstadter, who feels that the urban merchant, manufacturer, and lawyer, the civic leaders of an earlier era, and the old gentry entered the Progressive party in order to improve their decaying social positions.[1] His view seems to receive support from three surveys of Progressive leadership. Alfred D. Chandler has examined 260 Progressives and found them to be remarkably alike in urban residency, occupation, education, age, and family origin. George E. Mowry has also discovered striking social and economic similarities among 47 outstanding Progressives of California, and he has presented the same conclusions as to status in a nation-wide profile of 400 Progressives.[2]

Although the status revolution thesis may offer a partial explanation of insurgent behavior in 1912, it leaves unanswered two essential questions: Does the status of Progressives differentiate them from standpatters who continued to support the Republican party? Is it possible

1. See Richard Hofstadter, *The Age of Reform: From Bryan to F.D.R.* (New York, 1956).
2. A. D. Chandler, "The Origins of Progressive Leadership," in E. E. Morison (ed.), *The Letters of Theodore Roosevelt* (8 vols., Cambridge, 1951-54) VIII, 1462-65; G. E. Mowry, *The California Progressives* (Berkeley, 1952), and *The Era of Theodore Roosevelt* (New York, 1958).

32

that the leaders of both groups emanated from a common base in society? The answers can only be found in a considered analysis of the Old Guard.

When all statistics about the status of the Old Guard are compiled and compared with existing data on Progressive leaders, there remains one outstanding conclusion: in social and economic background regular Republicans strikingly resembled their progressive counterparts. It was primarily political experience that differentiated the two groups.

TABLE 1

REGIONAL DISTRIBUTION OF TAFT MEN

AREA	884 TAFT MEN		292 TAFT MEN	
	Number	Percentage	Number	Percentage
Northeast	241	27	81	28
Middle West	349	39	103	35
South	139	16	38	13
West	155	18	70	24

Of the statistics about Taft men, those concerning place of residence and occupation are based on my study of 884 men and women who gave their time and money to the regular Republican cause. Information relating to education, age, and political experience, which was more difficult to obtain, is based on a survey of the 292 most politically active Old Guardsmen. The geographical distribution of both groups is approximately the same (see Table 1).

Foremost among the similarities between regular and progressive leaders was their overwhelmingly urban and upper-middle-class origin. A majority of the Roosevelt supporters came from urban centers, while 60 per cent of the Taft men also lived in cities with populations of over 25,000, although the United States at the time was nearly 70 per cent rural.[3] Even in the South, 89 per cent rural and the most rural area of the country, 52 per cent of the Old Guard lived in cities (see Table 2).

Judged by their occupations, regulars and progressives were impressively middle class. At a time when professional groups were much smaller than today, more than half of the leading Roosevelt and Taft supporters were professional men. A majority of progressives were lawyers; nearly 20 per cent were newspapermen and editors, and the next largest group consisted of independent manufacturers and mer-

3. In 1910 the census bureau defined an urban area as a community of 2,500 or more. On this basis the United States was 46 per cent urban, while the 884 Taft men were 89 per cent urban.

chants. A small and active number of progressives were in other professions, but very few, if any, were farmers, laborers, or non-professional
white-collar workers.

Taft Republicans emanated from a similar narrow base in society (see
Table 3). Of the regulars 54 per cent were either businessmen, lawyers,
newspapermen, bankers, or financiers. About 6 per cent were scattered
in other professions; they included educators, clergymen, physicians,

TABLE 2

URBAN-RURAL DISTRIBUTION OF 884 TAFT MEN

AREA	TAFT MEN				UNITED STATES POPULATION	
	Number Urban	Number Rural	Percentage Urban	Percentage Rural	Percentage Urban	Percentage Rural
A. Urban based on population of 25,000 or more						
Northeast	165	76	68	32	51	49
Middle West	210	139	60	40	29	71
South	72	67	52	48	11	89
West	79	76	51	49	26	74
TOTAL	526	358	60	40	31	69
B. Urban based on population of 2,500 or more						
Northeast	222	19	92	8	71	29
Middle West	315	34	90	10	45	55
South	113	26	81	19	20	80
West	135	20	87	13	43	57
TOTAL	785	99	89	11	46	54

engineers, and authors. There were neither white-collar representatives,
laborers, nor farmers, although there were seven officials of agricultural
societies and seven labor union leaders. The one major differentiation
was the number of politicians in each group. While few progressive
leaders were professional politicians, almost 38 per cent of the regulars
earned their living as officeholders at either the federal, state, or local
level, and most of these men were also lawyers, businessmen, or newspapermen.

Old Guardsmen and progressives from all sections of the nation were
concerned with the interests of the business and professional community. Even in the predominantly rural areas the farmers were not the
party leaders, nor were union men the party representatives in the
industrial regions. Southern and western progressives tended to be aggressive entrepreneurs who were forming a new elite in society, while
northern progressives were generally from older, well-established families

and business enterprises. Those progressives who were in professions other than the law or business were concentrated largely in the cities of the North.

Taft supporters were very much like each other in all sections of the country, as no region had an outstandingly active group which came from any profession outside the law, the business, or the political community (see Table 4). In the South 54 per cent of the Taft leaders

TABLE 3

OCCUPATIONAL DISTRIBUTION OF 884 TAFT MEN

OCCUPATION	Northeast	AREA Middle West	South	West	Total
A. By number					
Businessmen	43	68	27	22	160
Lawyers	31	64	16	21	132
Newspapermen and Editors	37	59	6	17	119
Bankers and Financiers	27	23	5	12	67
TOTAL	138	214	54	72	478
Federal Officials	21	43	61	20	145
U. S. Senators and Representatives	32	41	9	29	111
State and Local Officials	22	26	5	16	69
TOTAL	75	110	75	65	325
Other*	17	18	4	11	50
Unknown	11	7	6	7	31
TOTAL	28	25	10	18	81
TOTAL IN AREA	241	349	139	155	884
B. By percentage					
Businessmen	4.9	7.7	3.0	2.5	18.1
Lawyers	3.5	7.2	1.8	2.4	14.9
Newspapermen and Editors	4.2	6.7	.7	1.9	13.5
Bankers and Financiers	3.0	2.6	.6	1.4	7.6
TOTAL	15.6	24.2	6.1	8.2	54.1
Federal Officials	2.4	4.9	6.9	2.3	16.5
U. S. Senators and Representatives	3.6	4.6	1.0	3.3	12.5
State and Local Officials	2.5	2.9	.6	1.8	7.8
TOTAL	8.5	12.4	8.5	7.4	36.8
Other*	1.9	2.0	.5	1.2	5.6
Unknown	1.2	.8	.7	.8	3.5
TOTAL	3.1	2.8	1.2	2.0	9.1
TOTAL PERCENTAGE IN AREA	27.2	39.4	15.8	17.6	100.0

*This category includes 15 educators, 7 agricultural officials, 7 labor union men, 6 clergymen, and 15 scattered among physicians, engineers, and authors.

35

were officeholders. Elsewhere the largest group of regulars were well-established businessmen, lawyers, newspapermen, and bankers. Regionally, the Taft men were more consistently similar than the progressives, but the majority in each group supported the tradition that American

TABLE 4

COMPARISON OF OCCUPATIONS OF 884 TAFT MEN

OCCUPATION	PERCENTAGE OF 241 TAFT MEN IN NORTHEAST	PERCENTAGE OF 349 TAFT MEN IN MIDDLE WEST	PERCENTAGE OF 139 TAFT MEN IN SOUTH	PERCENTAGE OF 155 TAFT MEN IN WEST
Businessmen	18	20	20	14
Lawyers	13	19	11	14
Newspapermen and Editors	15	17	4	11
Bankers and Financiers	11	6	4	8
TOTAL	57	62	39	47
Federal Officials	9	12	44	12
U. S. Senators and Representatives	13	12	6	19
State and local Officials	9	7	4	10
TOTAL	31	31	54	41
Other	7	5	3	7
Unknown	5	2	4	5
TOTAL	12	7	7	12

political leaders usually are lawyers, editors, and men of the established business community.

Regulars and progressives were strikingly similar to each other in their educational background. In 1912, when the proportion of college graduates was much smaller than today and a college degree ordinarily stamped a person as coming from the upper middle class, a majority of Taft and Roosevelt supporters were college graduates. Of the Roosevelt men, 50 to 75 per cent were college graduates; half of the most wealthy group attended Harvard, Princeton, and Yale. Sixty-three per cent of the Taft men were college graduates, and 22 per cent of them attended Ivy League schools (see Table 5). In addition, nearly 9 per cent were lawyers who had received their training without the benefit of a college education. Thus about 72 per cent of the Taft men had either graduated from college or had legal training.

The great majority of Old Guardsmen and progressives were native-born Protestants of Anglo-Saxon stock. A large proportion of both groups had names of British origin, while less than 5 per cent were foreign born. Few were Negroes. Generally, progressives were the reli-

TABLE 5

EDUCATIONAL DISTRIBUTION OF 292 TAFT MEN

EDUCATION	Northeast	AREA Middle West	South	West	Total
A. BY NUMBER					
Graduates of non-Ivy League Colleges	14	53	18	33	118
Graduates of Ivy League Colleges	41	13	3	8	65
Lawyers but not College Graduates	4	11	5	5	25
Without College or Legal Training	22	26	12	24	84
TOTAL IN AREA	81	103	38	70	292
TOTAL GRADUATES AND LAWYERS	59	77	26	46	208
B. BY PERCENTAGE					
Graduates of non-Ivy League Colleges	4.8	18.1	6.2	11.3	40.4
Graduates of Ivy League Colleges	14.0	4.5	1.0	2.7	22.2
Lawyers but not College Graduates	1.4	3.8	1.7	1.7	8.6
Without College or Legal Training	7.6	8.9	4.1	8.2	28.8
PERCENTAGE IN AREA	27.8	35.3	13.0	23.9	100.0
PERCENTAGE OF GRADUATES AND LAWYERS	20.2	26.4	8.9	15.8	71.3

gious descendants of Calvin and Knox, with the Congregationalists, Presbyterians, and Unitarians in the vast majority, but a significant number were Quaker women and wealthy Jews. Regular supporters presented a similar breakdown, except that women were much less important among the Taft supporters; only 4 of the 884 regulars were women. The largest number of Taft men were Presbyterians, Methodists, Congregationalists, and Unitarians. A number of Jews, who contributed large amounts of money to the Taft campaign, were influential in several urban areas outside the South, particularly in New York, San Francisco, and Cincinnati.

Taft men were virtually the same kind of people as their progressive antagonists in urban living, occupation, education, religion, and ethnic background. Nevertheless, there were significant differentiations in the age and political experience of the two groups, with regulars ten to fifteen years older on the average than the Roosevelt men. Progressives became prominent politically when they were young, generally between

thirty-five and forty-five years of age. The average age of the Taft supporters, fifty-four, varied little from region to region. The oldest Taft
men lived in the Northeast, where they averaged fifty-seven years of
age; the youngest came from the West, where they averaged fifty-two.

TABLE 6

POLITICAL EXPERIENCE OF 292 TAFT MEN

POLITICAL EXPERIENCE	AREA				
	Northeast	Middle West	South	West	Total
A. BY NUMBER					
Before 1900	47	66	25	39	177
After 1900	20	21	12	14	67
Without Experience	14	16	1	17	48
TOTAL IN AREA	81	103	38	70	292
TOTAL WITH POLITICAL EXPERIENCE	67	87	37	53	244
B. BY PERCENTAGE					
Before 1900	16.1	22.6	8.6	13.4	60.7
After 1900	6.8	7.2	4.1	4.8	22.9
Without Experience	4.8	5.5	.3	5.8	16.4
PERCENT. IN AREA	27.7	35.3	13.0	24.0	100.0
PERCENT. WITH POLITICAL EXPERIENCE	22.9	29.8	12.7	18.2	83.6

The average age of the 31 members of the executive and advisory boards
of the Republican National Committee was fifty-two.

The regulars were older not only in years but in political experience
as well. All but a handful of the Roosevelt men had previously been
Republicans, but they had little experience outside of local politics. On
the other hand, all of the regular leaders had been Republicans prior
to 1912, and nearly 38 per cent had made politics a full-time career (see
Table 6). Sixteen and a half per cent were federal appointees, 12.5 per
cent were members of the United States House or Senate, and nearly 8
per cent were state or local officials. Additionally, almost 84 per cent of
the Taft men had held some elective or appointive office. Over 60 per
cent had political experience pre-dating 1900.

The average Old Guard leader then, was an urban, upper-middle-class,
college-educated, native-born, Protestant who came from economically
and socially well-established, Anglo-Saxon stock. He was either a businessman, a lawyer, a newspaperman, or a politician, who at fifty-four
was a lifelong Republican with many years of political experience. He
was older and more accustomed to party discipline than his progressive
antagonist, but otherwise he was much the same.

Regular and progressive leaders, basically similar in background, were the elite of the Republican party. The difference in age and experience between the two groups, which wedded one to the establishment and the other to revolt, may also have had another significant effect. The older men, by and large satisfied with affairs, had reason to rationalize their support of the status quo. The younger, impatient for office and power, had need to criticize the existing order. The variations in the political attitudes of the Old Guard and of the progressives rested even more, of course, in genuine differences of conviction. And in the end, ideology—more than any other factor—accounted for the division, and even the hostility, between the rivals.

The fundamental attitude of the regulars toward man and society differentiated them in large measure from most progressive Republicans. The foundation of Old Guard ideology rested on the belief that man was base. Most regulars accepted as fact the idea that the sin and selfishness of mankind were nearly ineradicable. They found man to be an utterly selfish, insatiable creature whose appetite grew by what it fed upon and who was never content to say "enough." Old Guardsmen felt that the record of history too clearly demonstrated the presence of evil in the world and the pitiable weakness of human nature. The clearest spokesmen for the regular cause repeatedly referred to the depravity of human nature in their public statements. "Human nature does not change very much," Elihu Root maintained. "The forces of evil are hard to control now as they always have been. It is easy to fail and hard to succeed in reconciling liberty and order. . . . In the nature of things all government must be imperfect because men are imperfect."[4] President Nicholas Murray Butler of Columbia also believed that human nature was not going to change: "All the old passions, and desires, and ambitions, and weaknesses, and sins which have dogged the path of humanity from its first recorded appearance on earth are going to [continue to] pursue it."[5]

A corollary to the Old Guards' pessimistic conception of man was their view that inequality formed the inevitable basis of society. The very nature of man determined that some men were born to lead and most were born to be led. "Equality of ability, of efficiency, and even of physical force are unknown among men," Butler said. Continuing in a

4. Elihu Root, "Experiments in Government and the Essentials of the Constitution," *North American Review*, CXCVIII (July-August, 1913), 8, 10.
5. N. M. Butler, *Why Should We Change Our Form of Government?* (New York, 1912), 59.

Darwinian metaphor, he argued that the cornerstone of democracy was natural inequality, and its ideal was the selection of the most fit.[6] Taft also saw the development of civilization as a struggle involving the natural inequality of man. "The whole human race," he said, "has had to fight its way upward to modern civilization . . . by a struggle so arduous and so long continued that we can no more appreciate it than we can realize the time taken to create the geological formations." The "operation of natural laws" during this struggle gave us in some men "the virtues of providence, of industry, and of honesty and . . . all the other traits and virtues that we admire. . . ."[7] This doctrine permitted the Old Guard some degree of optimism about the future of America. "True democracy," Butler predicted, "will carry on an insistent search for these wisest and best, and will elevate them to posts of leadership and command. Under the operation of the law of liberty, it will provide itself with real leaders, not limited by rank, or birth, or wealth, or circumstance, but opening the way for each individual to rise to the place of honor and influence by the expression of his own best and highest self."[8] In spite of man's baseness, the regulars believed that society would progress under proper leadership.

According to this logic, only a natural aristocracy was equipped to lead society and to understand that moral considerations outweighed the mere blind struggle for existence in human affairs. Most Old Guardsmen were convinced that an elite would be guided, not by passion or expediency, but by high morality and duty to the public. In part the regulars preached such moral excellencies as justice, honesty, and service to avoid the dangers in their doctrine of the selfish, acquisitive man. Secretary of Commerce and Labor Charles Nagel thought that "every office and every institution should be an illustration of all we teach in our schools and preach in our churches. . . . Virtue and integrity," he said, "are practical, and will be admitted to be so as they become aggressive in their own cause."[9]

Most Old Guardsmen believed also that high moral behavior determined the socially and economically successful individual. Indeed, as a group they felt that only moral men could lift civilization to a higher plane and make democracy secure. The regulars anticipated principled behavior from the elite in large measure because of their own personal

6. N. M. Butler, *True and False Democracy* (New York, 1907), 9, 14-15, 57.
7. W. H. Taft, *Four Aspects of Civic Duty* (New York, 1906), 18-19.
8. Butler, *True and False*, 13.
9. Charles Nagel, *Speeches and Writings: 1900-1928*, ed. Otto Heller (2 vols., New York, 1931), I, 222.

experience. The memory of their parents endowed men like Butler, Root, Stimson, and Taft with an image of gentlefolk of the old school, who taught their sons to follow high standards in caring for public affairs. Butler remembered his father as a man who did his work thoroughly and who entered actively into the public life of the city of Paterson, the state of New Jersey, and the Republican party. "He took the keenest interest in the education of his children and followed with affectionate solicitude every step in the early career of each one of them."[10] Root remembered his father and the other professors at Hamilton College with great respect. They were men, Root said, "who sought for truth as one who strives in a game." They cared little for money, and they became accustomed to simple, sincere lives, made happy by the pleasures of intellect and taste. "For a boy to live with such men, to be close to them . . . to get their standards and become impressed by their estimates of the values of life, and to learn enough out of books in the meantime to understand it all—that is an education beyond price."[11] Of his father, Stimson said, "He was the man who of all others had the greatest influence upon the ideals and purposes of my adolescent life." Stimson noted that his father, a professor of surgery, was never particularly interested in the development of a lucrative private practice. "He lived frugally," Stimson recalled, and "throughout his life he maintained his love of the classics and of classical and European history."[12] Taft's father achieved success as a member of President Grant's Cabinet and as minister at Vienna and St. Petersburg. All the Taft children remembered his "moralistic aphorisms," his interest in their education, and his assurances of loyalty and affection. Upon the death of his father, Taft wrote to his wife, "I have a kind of presentment that Father has been a kind of guardian angel to me in that his wishes for my success have been so strong and intense as to bring it. . . ."[13]

The Old Guard's attachment to a governing elite stemmed not only from their doctrine of inequality; it developed, too, from a fear of mob action. Root said, "Men in mass are more irresponsible and difficult of control than individuals."[14] Taft believed that nothing could be more detrimental to the public interest than for any part of the people to take

10. N. M. Butler, *Across the Busy Years: Recollections and Reflections* (2 vols., New York, 1939), I, 37-38.
11. Quoted in P. C. Jessup, *Elihu Root* (2 vols., New York, 1938), I, 18-19, 21.
12. McGeorge Bundy and H. L. Stimson, *On Active Service in Peace and War* (New York, 1948), xvii.
13. Quoted in Pringle, *Taft*, I, 7, 16-17.
14. Root, "Experiments in Government," 272-73.

the law into their own hands. "Assembled in a mob," he maintained, "they soon lose their conscience; the spirit of the mob, different from that of any individual, enters the crowd; and the desire for vengeance prompts it to acts of violence and of the most fiendish cruelty."[15] The regulars believed that the people could turn into a mob when conditions pressed hardest for solution. It was then that the demogogue could destroy society by telling those who would listen that the voice of the people was the voice of God, and that it was better to trust the instincts and common sense of the masses than to follow expert guidance. When reason was unhinged by passion, and when appetite ruled the will, the people were the mob. Only when intelligent reflection asserted itself, and when action was based on principle, did the mob become the people. Because this line between the mob and the people was particularly narrow in a democracy, the regulars attached a heavy responsibility to elite leadership.

Elite leadership, according to the Old Guard position, had to ignore popularity as a guide to action. The representatives who made law, the judges who interpreted it, and the administrators who executed it had to maintain freedom from interference while they discharged their tasks. "If there is a weakness in representative bodies today," Nagel suggested, "it is their too ready response to superficial popular demand. The flood of suggestions for legislation constitutes nothing more nor less than the effort to please spasmodic popular feeling."[16] Taft was certain that the man from whom the people really secured the best service was the man who acted on his own judgment as to what was best for his country and for the people, even though this might be contrary to the temporary popular notion or passion. "The men who are really the great men of any legislative body," he said, "are those who, having views of their own, defend them and support them, even at the risk of rousing a popular clamor against themselves."[17] Butler maintained that the true democratic representative was not the "cringing, fawning tool of the caucus or of the mob, but he who, rising to the full stature of political manhood, does not take orders but offers guidance." A real leader of the people would not alter his course to meet "each shifting breeze of opinion or puff of passion."[18] Rather, he would be the spokesman for the conscience, the insight, and the judgment of the people as his own deep-

15. Taft, *Four Aspects*, 49.   16. Nagel, *Speeches*, I, 35.

17. Taft, *Popular Government: Its Essence, Its Permanance and Its Perils* (New Haven, 1913), 60-61.

18. Butler, *True and False*, 17-19.

est and sincerest conviction revealed them to him. American society had to provide itself with a foil of its own against the threat of rapid change, and none was better or more effective than a governing aristocracy.

Most progressives, contrary to the prevailing position of the regulars, were optimistic about society and man's place in it. Although they admitted that man had some bad habits, these progressives maintained that the Devil was not inherent in human nature. Evil existed primarily in society. It arose from inequality of opportunity and the hopelessness of an unequal struggle.

Since the progressives believed that basically all men were roughly alike in native ability and intelligence, many among them were antagonistic to the idea of elite leadership in American democratic society. A great body of progressives subscribed to a familiar American dogma about the democratic process. The near monopoly of leadership by the aristocracy, they felt, was due simply to the existence of social and economic inequalities which could be removed. No representative had the right to defeat the will of the people who elected him, they argued. Nothing should stand in the way of the voice of the people—not an aristocracy of the expert nor experience of the past.[19]

It seemed to the Old Guard that this dominant progressive attitude favored a leveling process in society which flaunted the laws of nature. Taft felt that it was essential that America's material progress should continue in order to meet the demands of a growing population and to increase general comfort. But, he added: "Were we to take away the selfish motive involved in private property we would halt, stagnate and then retrograde, the average comfort and happiness in society would be diminished, and those who are now in want would be poorer than ever."[20] Although the regulars placed a basic reliance on the political wisdom of the entire American people, they could not accept the common progressive notion that any American, regardless of training, was fit for any position in public life.

Republicans also disagreed about the inevitable progress of society. Old Guardsmen believed that nature imposed limitations upon what it was possible for man to accomplish or for government to regulate. "There is a line beyond which Government can not go with any good

19. This position not only contrasted with the Old Guard doctrine of a natural elite, but clashed as well with the views of a number of progressives, including Roosevelt, who believed that America needed a public-spirited aristocracy of intellect, service, and morality recruited from every part of society.

20. Taft, *Popular Government*, 229.

practical results in seeking to make men and society better," Taft said.[21] Any willingness of the Old Guard to experiment with change usually emanated from a desire to see that injustices were not permitted to become so deep as to arouse the spirit of revolt. "If the abuses of monopoly and discrimination can not be restrained; if the concentration of power made possible by such abuses continues and increases, and it is made manifest that under the system of individualism and private property the tyranny and oppression of an oligarchy of wealthy can not be avoided," Taft warned, "then socialism will triumph and the institution of private property will perish."[22] In most cases approval of reform merely reflected the Old Guard attachment to the existing order. The Old Guard way to make real progress and to retain permanently each advance was to move wisely along legitimate political lines. The regulars believed that the natural development of an ordered society was itself the promise of progress.

While a great body of progressives never considered themselves radical and resisted what seemed to them revolutionary, they usually welcomed change. "Perhaps it is best to 'bear the ills we have rather than fly to those we know not of,' " one progressive editor wrote to an Old Guard friend, "but for myself I prefer to take up the problems of the day in the light we now have rather than that of the past. . . . The world moves and we have got to move with it. . . . So with all that is going on in politics today. . . . It is evolution, and not revolution."[23] Regulars saw the prelude to social disaster in this position.

In the debate over political ideology, economic questions sank into the background. The tariff, railroad regulation, and conservation, which had nearly consumed Republican energies from 1909 to 1911, paled before the issues of popular democracy. Intra-party dissent over economic matters continued to plague the Republicans, but these disagreements did not follow a clear factional line. Regulars and progressives split internally in their position on the economic purpose of government, with large segments in each camp both in favor and in fear of economic change.

Because they saw in the economic world a natural order which permitted man to rearrange his material environment with some success, most regulars accepted change in the economic field more readily than

21. Taft, *Popular Government*, 35.
22. Taft, *Popular Government*, 46.
23. H. L. Stoddard to J. R. Sheffield, July 25, 29, 1912, William Rockwell Sheffield Papers, Yale University Library.

in the realm of politics. Many Old Guardsmen and progressives agreed generally on the need for some kind of federal economic regulation, even though they were not in accord on a specific legislative program. Indeed, regulars often approved of federal regulation of tariffs, monopolies, natural resources, taxes, and banking, while they argued against impractical changes in law and government. Thus Butler could maintain at one time that every immediate demand for political action had to be tested as to its validity by the standard of the fundamental principles of organized government to which the American people gave allegiance. "Every departure from it," he said, "every outburst against it, every violation of it is not American; it is anti-American, abnormal and pathologic."[24] Yet at another moment Butler could endorse federal regulation of competition. "What happens in every form of organic evolution is that an old part no longer useful to the structure drops away, and its functions pass over into and are absorbed by a new development," Butler said. "That new development is cooperation, and cooperation as a substitute for unlimited, unrestricted, individual competition has come to stay as an economic fact, and legal institutions will have to be adjusted to it. It cannot be stopped. It ought not to be stopped. It is not in the public interest that it should be stopped."[25] Important elements among regulars and progressives believed that the government was duty bound to protect society from monopolies which threatened free competition, and they approved of federal efforts to restore economic liberty and equality of opportunity. Even the most conservative Old Guardsmen thought that government should discharge a general service when private enterprise could not do so effectively. "Everyone of us must recognize that the days of pure individualism are gone," Nagel admitted. "We confess that there is a certain proportion of people who cannot keep up with the procession, who are bound to fall by the wayside, and to whom government must extend its care."[26]

The opposition to the concept of government as an instrument of economic action came similarly from both Republican camps. Numbers of both regulars and progressives believed that undue government interference with individual liberty and property would destroy independence of character in the American citizenry. They feared that forceful leadership and federal responsibility would cultivate a corrupting paternalism under a bureaucratic government.

24. N. M. Butler, *The American As He Is* (New York, 1908) 29-30.
25. Butler, *Why Should We Change?* 81-82.
26. Nagel, *Speeches*, I, 235.

Political thought, particularly when compared with economic views, was a fundamental ingredient of Old Guard distinctiveness. Regular Republican leaders held to a general political faith which, in their own opinion, irreconcilably separated them from progressive Republicans. The major tenets of this Old Guard credo were the (1) certainty of man's baseness, (2) persistence of natural inequality in society, (3) inevitability of elite leadership, (4) importance of high morality, (5) limitation of progress by natural laws, (6) folly of change except in the economic realm, (7) reverence for past experience, (8) fear of mob action and popular democracy, (9) necessity for stability of representative institutions, and (10) sanctity of constitutionalism, law, and the courts.

Men with a considerable variety in their political views supported the Old Guard credo. Typical of the center of this wide range was Attorney General George W. Wickersham, whose extreme reverence for the law was counterbalanced by his insistence on federal regulation, especially in economic matters. Slightly to his left were men like Butler and the President, whose desires for social justice exceeded those of most Old Guardsmen. Senator Root, who upheld the sanctity of the Constitution while grudgingly conceding the need for some reform under elite leadership, personified those who stood to the right of center. Secretaries Nagel and Stimson represented the most extreme wings of the Old Guard political spectrum. Nagel looked with distress at increased government bureaucracy and the trend to over-legislation. Stimson supported Taft because he thought the President had done well in leading Republicans and the nation toward progressive goals. For his own part Stimson could see no essential difference between Roosevelt and Taft, except in their personalities and in their positions on recall of judicial decisions. While Nagel thought that Republicanism alone could restore the permanent virtues of the American past, Stimson believed that the party was the best hope for the advancement of American society.

Although the political credo of the Old Guard was elastic enough to allow variations in thought—an essential requisite for a national party organization—regular leaders, on the whole, maintained a conservative ideology. On a political scale even the most radical supporters of the President stood to the right of most progressives. Stimson's belief in federal responsibility, for example, placed him to the far left within the Old Guard ranks, but his attitudes toward law, constitutionalism, and representative democracy reflected the conservative influence of Senator Root, with whom he had experienced close legal and personal associations. Stimson was at best a progressive conservative. However

46

the supporters of regular Republicanism emphasized the points of their political faith, they agreed that the essential institution of American society was governmental stability and that without it a free United States was impossible.

Ideology affected the actions of many Old Guardsmen, who cherished their political faith although they rarely explored it. Numbers of prominent regulars, including Hilles, accepted the conservative position without endeavoring to formalize it in writing or oratory. Indeed, as a group, the regulars were among the least articulate of public men. The epitome of silence was Senator Crane. One of the most important party leaders, he never uttered a word in Senate debate during his ten years of office. Even Secretary Nagel did not begin to arrange his thoughts until 1912, when the progressives challenged his somewhat vague beliefs. Except for Taft and Butler, no Old Guardsmen attempted consciously and continually to set forth a credo. This want of philosophic rhetoric reflected the dominant place in the Old Guard of the professional politician, whose primary concerns were immediate and practical. Unlike the progressives, the ranks of the regulars did not contain significant numbers of authors or professors. The leaders of the Old Guard were neither eloquent nor intellectual.

The cause of popular reform and the means to good government were the basic issues of the Republican division. The Old Guard wholeheartedly believed in the stability of American political institutions. They felt that only with governmental orderliness, respect for law, and the maintenance of the Constitution was it possible to preserve the American way of life. In their view nothing presented a more immediate danger to existing political stability than the proposals for popular democracy which the progressives supported. The regulars thought that the reform movement, initially directed against intolerable conditions and individualism run wild, had deviated from its origins. Impetus was one thing; direction was quite another. The spirit of protest, no longer content to correct unjust practices, seemed girded for a radical change of American political institutions.

With the endorsement of a trio of reform measures—the initiative, the referendum, and the recall of judicial decisions—the progressive program appeared to the Old Guard to have assumed the character of a crusade with socialistic tendencies. The progressives seemed, in effect, to be proposing a false system of American life, which demanded that every man in society be brought to an average level. Taft believed that the implementation of initiative, referendum, and recall would lead to

47

the extinction of competition, which was part of the struggle for existence and for success. The natural inequalities, without which the process
of evolution could not continue, would be wiped out. Taft considered
these prospects to be un-American and even socialistic: "The ultimate
issue is socialism and an unlimited control of the majority of the electorate on the one hand, or our present government on the other. . . ."[27]

The Old Guard feared especially the consequences to law if the progressive attitude successfully permeated American society. The regulars
had a deep reverence for law, which they considered the greatest single
aid to governmental stability. Many regulars believed that law was the
expression of the will of God and the manifestation of right and justice.
In all human institutions, statutes reached out to establish justice and to
insure domestic tranquility. Yet it seemed to the Old Guard that the progressives were making a mockery of the law. Without considering the
negative results, progressives had come to accept the idea that there was
a legislative cure for every ill—political, industrial, or social. "We are
in truth," Attorney General Wickersham lamented, "a law ridden people."[28] Popular reformers impatiently demanded statutes one day and
defied them the next with equal impatience. This vacillation threatened
to destroy public confidence in law and to create a grave danger to
America from a generation which no longer revered and regarded law
as the key to a civilized state and free institutions. The progressives appeared to have dimissed a concept which the regulars kept foremost in
their thought: Statutes themselves changed, but the principles underlying
the existence of law did not and could not change unless society were to
be destroyed.

Another calamitous result the Old Guard anticipated from political
reform was the destruction of the American Constitution. The regulars
held the Constitution in high esteem because it embodied for them the
conclusions of some of the wisest, purest, and best men of history as to
what was necessary for the preservation of liberty, justice, and order.
Their interpretation of the Constitution served as sheet-anchor of the
conservative principle and, with its expressed limitations and division
of power, provided a model of self-restraint in the practical conduct of
life. The document also showed the regulars that, where power was
greatest and where men acted in mass, self-restraint was the supreme
necessity and the supreme virtue of government. Thus the Old Guard
condemned any suggestion to alter the Constitution, except by amend-

27. Taft, *Popular Government*, 95.
28. G. W. Wickersham, *The Changing Order* (New York, 1914), 34.

ment, as hideous folly and a direct attack on the principles of nature. Many Republicans supported the regular party primarily because they believed it to be the best protector of the Constitution.

What brought the ideological differentiation on popular reform into sharp focus was the tone of Roosevelt's address in the state constitutional convention at Columbus, Ohio, on February 21, 1912. In this speech, entitled "A Charter for Democracy," Roosevelt declared his hat in the ring for the Republican presidential nomination, and he espoused the cause of popular democracy. Roosevelt was moderate enough to appeal to many conservatives of the Republican party in his assurances to the business world and in his limited support of the initiative, referendum, and recall of judges. His total support of the recall of judicial decisions in state courts, however, and his attack on American judicial institutions alienated the Old Guard almost to a man. Roosevelt took special issue with those Republicans who believed that the American people were not fitted for popular government and who said that the judiciary had to be kept independent of the majority of the people. Roosevelt insisted that when a judge decided a constitutional question, when he decided what the people as a whole could or could not do, the people had the right to recall that decision if they thought it wrong. If the courts had the final word on all legislative acts, and if there were no appeal from them to the people, then the courts would be irresponsible masters of the people. "We should hold the judiciary in all respect," Roosevelt maintained, "but it is both absurd and degrading to make a fetich of a judge or of anyone else."[29]

Taft replied to Roosevelt's declaration in an address at Toledo on March 9. His remarks well represented the Old Guard position. Without mentioning Roosevelt by name, the President characterized the recall of judicial decisions as crude and utterly without merit. The President maintained that although judges performed a governmental function, to assume that they were bound to follow the will of a majority of an electorate was a complete misunderstanding of American government, or any kind of government that exalted justice. Reformers thought fallaciously that because the people were competent to establish a constitution, they were qualified to interpret it. What a remarkable suggestion it was, Taft said, that the electorate should have the power to invalidate the decision of a court! Judicial recall was a method of amending the Constitution which gave that great document no more permanence than an ordinary legislative act and no more sanction than an annual appro-

29. New York *Tribune*, February 22, 1912.

priation bill. "It lays the axe at the foot of the tree of well ordered free-dom and subjects the guarantees of life, liberty and property without remedy to the fitful impulses of a temporary majority of the electorate." Instead of being progressive, the President said, judicial recall was re-actionary; instead of being in the interest of all the people and of the stability of popular government, it was sowing the seeds of confusion and tyranny.[30]

Roosevelt's endorsement of the recall of judicial decisions drove from him many Republicans who, for the sake of party victory, might other-wise have supported his presidential bid. Typical of this group was New York lawyer James R. Sheffield. "Feeling as I do," he wrote George Perkins, with "my regard for the orderly way of settling controversies, and especially those which involve constitutional questions . . . I must cast my lot on *this* issue with those who are opposed to the recall of judges and judicial decisions. I should do this even if I knew Colonel Roosevelt was to be nominated and elected; and I make this statement in order that you may know how deeply I feel upon these questions. I have not changed my personal regard for him in the slightest degree. I deeply regret his position on these public questions which makes it, for the first time, impossible for me to follow him."[31] A number of Roosevelt's close friends, including Root, Stimson, Lodge, and his own son-in-law, Ohio Congressman Nicholas Longworth, announced their opposition to the former President after his Columbus speech. The severest antagonism to Roosevelt developed among Old Guardsmen, who felt that the recall, above all other issues, epitomized the excesses of popular democracy. After the Columbus speech, the Old Guard admiration and devotion to the courts became almost mystical, and the regulars rallied behind Presi-dent Taft, who confided happily to his brother Horace that he saw a revolution of feeling in his favor among conservative men everywhere in the United States.

The impact of Roosevelt's progressivism helped to unite the Old Guard in the conviction that direct interference with an independent judiciary and representative institutions was not the answer to social and economic abuse. Although most regulars admitted the validity of the general prin-ciple of popular government, and in the long run placed their faith in democracy, they considered themselves to be republicans rather than democrats. Granting some evils in the representative system, the Old Guard felt that the whole tendency of progressive reform was to give a

30. New York *Tribune*, March 9, 1912.
31. J. R. Sheffield to G. W. Perkins, March 16, 1912, Sheffield Papers.

transient majority the right to tamper with the government, which was the cornerstone of the political fabric.

The issues of judicial recall and reform did not affect all Republicans in the same degree. Ideas were secondary to the quest for office for most party bosses and political hacks. The Republican struggle was for them primarily a scramble for seats of power rather than a contest between political faiths. The primary objectives of these men were to protect their own positions of influence and to prevent younger men from dominating party councils. Old-time Republicans opposed any measures of popular democracy, such as direct primaries, which threatened to change party structure. Unconcerned about the effect of reform measures on representative government, they paid little heed to comments from Taft, Butler, or Nagel. Party bosses objected to direct nominations because of their certainty that this method jeopardized their leadership, relegated old workers to the discard, and destroyed feelings of party loyalty and enthusiasm. Similarly, some of the progressive leaders had no intellectual conviction in the reform program but were governed instead by political expediency. Walter Brown in Ohio, William Flinn in Pennsylvania, and C. H. Campbell in Indiana supported Roosevelt in order to satisfy their aspirations for office or to recoup their political prestige at home. Not creed but patronage, not service but office, determined the loyalty of many Republicans.

Yet most of the support for Taft emanated from men whose conservative convictions outweighed their own desires for political entrenchment. The regulars, on the whole, were most concerned with the maintenance of stability through natural and constitutional law. They believed that progressive demands for reform constituted a direct attack on the American system of government. Most conservatives rallied behind Taft in order to preserve constitutional progress, to keep faith with the lessons of the past, and to defend American society from what they considered the dangerous excesses of popular democracy.

4. THE OLD GUARD
ORGANIZATION

Republican division, increasingly evident before 1912, became acute when Roosevelt entered the presidential campaign. His open declaration rallied progressives throughout the nation while intensifying the Old Guard's determination to retain party control. No regular recognized the danger of Roosevelt's candidacy more immediately than Taft. "The truth is," the President wrote early in March, "that the crisis is on now from this time until the Convention—the real crisis for conservative men."[1]

The very reason for Taft's remaining in a contest which he found personally distasteful was to save the Republican party from Roosevelt's brand of progressivism. Taft predicted that Roosevelt's nomination would place an ultra-radical at the head of the ticket and force the Democrats to nominate a radical as well. The campaign would become a chase to see which man could put his flag on the most extreme battlement of radicalism. It would disrupt Republicanism, he thought, and there was no knowing when the party might get together again for the purpose of reasserting its proper position in government, that of progressive conservatism. Taft was not quite sure which would be more disastrous, in case of Roosevelt's nomination—the election of a Democrat or a Republican. The President believed, however, that "if I were nominated, even though I were to go down to defeat, I should be on a conservative platform and should rally the conservative forces of this country and keep them in a nucleus of party strength, so that after four years the party could gather itself together and probably re-establish itself in control."[2]

In order to gain renomination, the President leaned almost entirely on the Old Guard for his support, much to the dismay of some of his associates. Secretary of the Treasury Franklin MacVeagh wanted the President to do everything that was fair to encourage and enlist the progressives. It was of great importance, he believed, that among the President's political advisers there should be as many representatives of the progressive element of the party as possible, to give the public mind a good impression. "If there is any tendency or purpose anywhere among the President's friends to corral his candidacy within the territory of

1. Taft to C. H. Clark, March 5, 1912, Hilles Papers.
2. *Ibid.*

the regulars," he said, "it ought to be discouraged and prevented. . . . I have always keenly realized and have constantly assumed in all my utterances, that the President is the real leader of the progressives; and that, at the same time, he is the leader of his whole party."[3] Yet Taft was of another mind. He was certain that his cause could be served best through regular party members.

More than ever Taft relied on Hilles to pursue vigorously conservative advantages. Although not so named officially, Hilles became the chief of the Taft organization; his major adviser was Senator Crane. Representative McKinley acted as the head of the Taft campaign, serving in a dual capacity as chairman of the Republican Campaign Committee and chairman of the Taft Bureau. The main headquarters of the Taft Bureau was located in Washington, with an eastern branch in New York and a western in Chicago. Working in close cooperation with Hilles, McKinley confined the activities of his bureau to publicity. Each day the Taft Bureau supplied a list of elected delegates for the press, quoted encouraging news from supporters, and mailed campaign literature to constituents. The Taft Bureau issued twice a week a pamphlet called "Taft Truths," advising the delegates on the progress of the campaign. It particularly attended to the Negro voters in the North and mailed thousands of pamphlets to colored citizens. Two other agencies worked in close harmony with Hilles and the Taft Bureau. The National League of Taft Clubs organized citizens into city and state booster clubs. The president of the league, Johns Hays Hammond, a wealthy engineer, traveled extensively and had agents especially active in New Hampshire, Massachusetts, New Jersey, and Georgia. Louis Hammerling, the president of the American Association of Foreign Newspapers, headed another agency which concentrated its attention on various ethnic groups. Hammerling coordinated the publicity which was filtered to the non-English press, and he guided the Taft appeal to the naturalized citizen. Most of his activity concerned German, eastern European, and Jewish voters. The three Taft organizations and their sub-agencies were directly responsible to Hilles. Generally, each agency held its activity within the limits prescribed for it by the secretary. There was almost no dissension among the men responsible for these agencies, and there was very little duplication of effort among the agencies.

The Roosevelt organization, on the other hand, feverishly constructed a nation-wide political system. Senator Joseph M. Dixon of Montana became the chairman of a national executive committee, which set up

3. Franklin MacVeagh to Hilles, March 11, 1912, Hilles Papers.

headquarters in New York and Chicago. The Roosevelt organization also established a press bureau and related committees, but despite this structure there was inefficiency and friction.

Since Hilles' organizational work in 1911 and 1912 placed Roosevelt at a disadvantage, especially in the South, the Roosevelt followers planned to put Taft's early delegate lead in question by discrediting the President's southern victories. Shortly after he became Roosevelt's campaign manager, Senator Dixon asserted that many doubtful delegations were being credited to Taft by his managers. He insisted that not more than half of the initial hundred southern delegates claimed for Taft were actually certain to support the President. In March Dixon announced that contests would be raised in all southern states because officeholders had controlled the call of most conventions by fraudulent tactics. He formally acknowledged that Ormsby McHarg was the political strategist for the South, and maintained that convincing proof of illegality would be presented to the national committee by the delegates instructed for Roosevelt. Dixon asked, "Do the Taft managers want to force an empty nomination at the Chicago convention at the point of bayonet?"[4]

Roosevelt's old agents, who had been close to him before 1908, began to serve their former chief again. Together with disgruntled politicians, they contested the Taft delegates and called rump conventions which selected pro-Roosevelt delegates. The Roosevelt leaders also challenged Taft to a primary contest in every state. By this strategy they hoped to influence primary legislation under consideration in several states and to make it appear that Taft was the candidate of machine politicians, while Roosevelt was the popular choice of the party's rank and file. Early in March Dixon called upon Congressman McKinley to join him in securing primary legislation in Massachusetts, Maryland, and Michigan, where such bills were pending and where, he said, friends of the President were trying to defeat their passage. If McKinley refused, Dixon maintained, it would reflect the President's fear of the voters as well as his willingness to become a candidate against the wishes of the majority of his party. Taft headquarters replied that it was too late to institute nation-wide primaries and that it would be unfair to change rules in the middle of the game since the national committee had declined to require the direct choice of delegates. It was extravagant and unwarranted to hold Taft enthusiasts responsible for the neglect of some states to equip themselves with direct election machinery. That fault rested entirely with

4. New York *Tribune*, March 16, 17, 1912.

the people of those states and could not be remedied by any action Mc-Kinley or Dixon might take.[5]

The question of nation-wide presidential primaries raised by Dixon turned into a public debate between Roosevelt and Taft. Roosevelt denounced McKinley's attitude in an open letter to Dixon, charging that practically the entire body of professional politicians was pitted against him and that only that group was opposed to a primary test. Furthermore, Roosevelt said, it was idle to insist that it was too late to make a change. Whenever men had failed to get the primary system, it was due to the work of reactionaries, who thoroughly distrusted the people and whose one aim was to prevent them from controlling the party organizations to which they belonged. Taft answered Roosevelt in a speech at Boston on April 25. While favoring primaries, the President insisted that full and fair notice had to be given in order to provide legal guarantees against election frauds. An immediate nation-wide contest would be nothing but a "soap box" primary, he said, which would open the way to chaos. The direct election method was spreading rapidly, Taft pointed out, and soon it would be the majority method. But it was foolish to talk of forcing primaries offhand at thirty days notice on states and districts which had not qualified under the protection of the law.[6]

After Taft's speech, the President's supporters fought fiercely almost everywhere against the adoption of direct election laws. Primary measures became law during the next two months in Illinois, Massachusetts, and Maryland, but similar proposals failed in Colorado, Kansas, Michigan, Minnesota, and Washington.

When the first three state primary elections, in March, resulted in defeats for Roosevelt, it appeared that perhaps Roosevelt had overestimated his popular appeal. Recognizing the President's unpopularity among North Dakota farmers because of his stand on Canadian reciprocity, the Taft managers made no effort to secure the delegation. The North Dakota primary on March 19 was strictly a contest between Roosevelt and La Follette. La Follette defeated Roosevelt in the statewide contest by 11,000 votes and secured all of the state's ten delegates. The regulars took great heart from the results. One Taft supporter wrote, "The impression prevails here that when North Dakota kicked Teddy's hat out of the ring, Teddy was sitting in his hat."[7]

Taft defeated Roosevelt in the Indiana primaries, which followed on

5. New York *Tribune*, March 7, 9, 1912.
6. New York *Tribune*, March 11, 12, 19, 1912.
7. G. F. Authier to E. E. Smith, March 19, 1912, Hilles Papers.

March 24. The elections were not a direct contest since Republicans voted for delegates to the district conventions and the state convention. But the Indiana campaign revealed a well-organized progressive machine. Harry S. New confessed his utter amazement early in the month at the way the Roosevelt sentiment had come to the front since the former President announced his candidacy. Roosevelt supporters, he said, "just seem to have arisen out of the grass and the bushes and to have overrun everything and everybody. I am convinced that so far as popular sentiment is concerned Roosevelt occupies the same position in the Republican party that Bryan does in the Democratic party, a great majority of the rank and file being for each of them." New reported to Hilles that the Roosevelt manager had beyond all question dumped a great deal of money into Indiana, and New began to wonder whether the President could control the state delegation. "If we win," he said, "it will be because of the organization." Every district chairman was for the President and would be found steadfast to the end. On the day before the primaries New telegraphed Hilles that the outlook was not favorable, and the next day he telegraphed, "We are still having an awful fight. . . ."[8] Yet the Taft forces won a majority of delegates to thirteen district conventions and to the Indiana state convention, while Roosevelt secured a majority only to the remaining five district conventions. Taft was, therefore, assured twenty delegates to the national convention, and Roosevelt ten. The Roosevelt managers immediately cried fraud, claimed that the primaries had not been conducted fairly, and promised to send several contesting delegations to the national convention. Former Senator James A. Hemenway remarked that the attitude of the Roosevelt managers to presidential primaries depended wholly on the question of whose ox was gored, and the Taft camp rejoiced that the President could win in a primary. Harry New heaved a sigh of relief: "I never was so glad to get anything behind me in all my life. . . ."[9]

Taft victory in the New York primaries came two days later on March 26. The election was no measure of Roosevelt's popularity because the New York primary law was so framed that the power to select delegates remained in the hands of the politicians. Weeks before the primaries the Old Guard assured itself of success. With William Barnes acting as director of policy in upstate areas and Samuel S. Koenig at the head of the Taft forces in New York City, the regulars gained control of most of the

8. H. S. New to Hilles, March 3, 23, 24, 1912, Hilles Papers.
9. New York *Tribune*, March 17, 19, 20, 1912; H. S. New to Hilles, March 26, 1912, Hilles Papers.

district committees. During the early part of March one committee after another nominated pro-Taft delegates on the Republican ticket. The only recourse for Roosevelt backers was to nominate their delegates by petition as independent candidates. Without the stamp of the Republican label the Roosevelt candidates faced almost certain defeat in the district primaries. Before the elections Roosevelt assailed the primary law and the Old Guard leaders who opposed him. He claimed that never had he seen patronage used more barefacedly than in New York. Koenig countercharged that many of the Roosevelt petitions were fradulent because they contained false signatures. The nominees running under Roosevelt's emblem, he said, were without exception the same disgruntled men who had been making the attempt for several years. As expected, Taft captured the New York delegation eighty-one to nine.[10]

By the first week in April the Roosevelt boom appeared to have run its course, and the Taft camp was certain of victory. Taft men claimed 344 delegates, while Roosevelt was certain of only 44 uncontested delegates. In addition, La Follette claimed 36 delegates and Cummins 10. Conditions in Iowa unquestionably added to the confidence in the Taft camp. John T. Adams and Frank Nimocks continued their successful organization of district leaders. All the districts held their conventions by the first week in April, with Taft winning in six conventions and Cummins in five. The Taft men also appeared certain to control a majority of delegates to the state convention on April 24, assuring the President of 16 of the 26 Iowa delegates to the national convention.

This optimism among Taft supporters was premature. Although the initial pre-convention activity favored Taft, it indicated that Roosevelt had latent strength. The primaries and southern contests showed that Roosevelt could rely on progressive organizations at the state and local level and on old friends of political influence. Roosevelt also appeared to have the whole-hearted endorsement of many rank-and-file progressives.

Overly confident, the Taft partisans predicted easy victory for the President in the Illinois and Pennsylvania primaries. Taft remained at the White House, while Roosevelt took to the stump. As progressive organizations moved into smooth operation, Roosevelt lashed out severely at Taft. In Illinois he linked Taft's name with Senator William Lorimer, who had been dismissed from his Senate seat because of involvement in corrupt practices. In Pennsylvania he suggested that a vote for Taft was

10. New York *Tribune*, March 3, 5, 8, 9, 17, 1912; S. S. Koenig to Taft, March 21, 1912, Hilles Papers.

a vote for Senator Penrose and bossism. On April 9 Roosevelt defeated Taft in Illinois by 140,000 votes; he gained 56 of the 58 delegates. On April 13 Roosevelt obtained a majority of 60,000 in Pennsylvania; he received 67 delegate votes, while Taft won 9. Shortly after the primaries, Taft admitted privately that his dual defeat was very significant in the hold which Roosevelt still had over the plain people. No explanation of the result was sufficient, he said, which did not make this the chief element.[11]

Encouraged by the results in Illinois and Pennsylvania, pro-Roosevelt sentiment gained momentum. On April 19 Taft was defeated in the Nebraska and Oregon primaries. The President came in third behind Roosevelt and La Follette in both contests, and Roosevelt gained 36 delegates. Victor Rosewater of Nebraska had predicted defeat a few days earlier, when he warned the President that it was idle for regulars to shut their eyes to the unfavorable influence of what had happened in Illinois and Pennsylvania.[12]

Roosevelt's growing strength had a deleterious effect on Old Guardsmen, but it intensified the President's own determination. Taft refused to settle for anything less than unconditional regular victory. The President made his position very clear late in April, when he intervened in the Missouri campaign. The Republicans of Missouri, who had achieved their first state victory in forty years with the election of Governor Herbert S. Hadley in 1909, were anxious to maintain a united front against the Democrats. This concern with state affairs was largely responsible for confusion in Republican ranks. Several times in March and April some of the regulars tried to appease the Roosevelt enthusiasts, led by Governor Hadley, in order to create harmony for the coming state elections. The animosity between Old Guard State Committeemen Otto F. Stifel and E. L. Morse and the regular chairman of the state committee, C. D. Morris, centered largely about the question of compromise with the governor. Morse and Stifel opposed any division of the delegates-at-large between Taft and Roosevelt and favored an all-out fight with Hadley. Chairman Morris believed that Governor Hadley was an important figure in Missouri affairs, and that it might pay to adjust differences with him. Secretary Nagel, whose home was in St. Louis, agreed with Morris. However much Taft's friends opposed the governor's posi-

11. F. L. Smith to Hilles, April 8, 1912, W. E. Mason to Hilles, April 11, 1912, J. C. Delaney to Hilles, April 23, 1912, Hilles Papers; Taft to Horace Taft, April 14, 1912, Taft Papers.
12. Victor Rosewater to W. B. McKinley, April 14, 1912, Hilles Papers.

tion on national questions, Nagel said, the Republican party of Missouri would naturally be slow to humiliate a man who had been enthusiastically supported and in many ways made a leader.[13]

When Taft learned that the Missouri state chairman was preparing to cooperate with Hadley and sacrifice delegates at the state convention, he acted immediately. The President wired the Old Guard leaders that he was against any compromise with the Roosevelt men.[14] As a consequence of Taft's position and the strength of the progressives, Hadley carried the convention. In addition to the loss of the 4 delegates-at-large, Taft lost four district conventions in April. The result of the bitter Missouri conventions was that the Taft forces claimed 20 of the 36 delegates. The Roosevelt supporters, not content with 16 delegates, contested Taft men in five districts.

In keeping with his non-compromise position, the President decided to wage a vigorous campaign. Over the protests of Senator Crane and Secretary Stimson, who thought that Taft should not attack Roosevelt personally, the President delivered a fighting speech at Boston on April 25, just five days before the Massachusetts primary. This speech set the tone for the remainder of the pre-convention campaign. It reaffirmed the President's view that he alone was the hope against radicalism and demagogy. "It is my duty," he told his brother Horace "to secure the nomination, if I can, under the rules that the Republican party convention has established, in spite of all threats to bolt or to establish a third party."[15]

During the late stages of the pre-convention campaign, Hilles found it increasingly difficult to weld together factions within the Old Guard. In California the Taft supporters split into two camps—the official Taft organization, composed of Old Guard leaders and headed by Charles Mifflin Hammond, and the "Progressives for Taft," led by Charles W. Hornick of the San Francisco *Call*. Despite several attempts to harmonize their activities, the two groups were not able to work together. Hornick explained that thousands of Republicans regarded Taft as a true progressive of accomplishment. Such men wanted to be for Taft, but they could not be made to do politics with the men they had driven out of the official life of the state. The "Progressives for Taft" suspended

13. C. D. Morris to Taft, April 4, 1912, Charles Nagel to Hilles, April 4, 1912, Hilles Papers.
14. Taft to T. J. Akins, April 20, 1912, Hilles Papers.
15. W. M. Crane to Hilles, April 20, 1912, Hilles Papers; H. L. Stimson, "Diary," 1910-13, 74, Stimson Papers; Taft to Horace Taft, April 14, 1912, Taft Papers.

their organization late in March.[16] During April the Taft situation deteriorated as the result of the primary defeats in Illinois, Pennsylvania, Oregon, and Nebraska. At the end of the month Old Guard Congressman Joseph R. Knowland admitted that the regular organization had gone to pieces.[17] A week before the primary, held on May 14, Hornick told Hilles that his heart was broken because he could see nothing but defeat for the President. Hammond was a gentleman born and bred, Hornick said, but he was a babe in politics. "Inexperience in California politics added to by the objectionable and poor timber he [Hammond] has surrounded himself with, has spoiled the magnificent fighting chance we had to carry California for Taft."[18] Taft carried one district and 2 delegates in the state primaries, while Roosevelt swept the rest of California and won 24 delegates.

An intense struggle for the 40-vote Texas delegation added to the President's difficulties. The chief obstacle in Texas was Cecil Lyon, the deposed referee, who used his patronage power to fight desperately for control of the Texas delegation. Early in March the Taft manager, H. F. MacGregor, traveled to every district in Texas in the company of Joseph Kealing, the aide sent by Hilles to help secure the Texas situation. MacGregor reported that nearly every district would be contested. Nevertheless, he was sure that the proceedings in all the districts would warrant the national committee in seating the Taft delegates. In April MacGregor and Kealing again made the long tour of the Texas districts in order to impress the district chairmen with the fact that, according to the express authority of the President, Lyon had no patronage power. They succeeded thereby in forcing every recalcitrant chairman to issue a call for conventions. The fight for delegates began in mid-April. "I cannot help but feel," MacGregor wrote on April 16, "that the real fight is over, for when we succeeded in getting these conventions called, we have reason to believe that the large majority of them will send instructed Taft delegates." The district conventions and the state convention, held in May, returned 31 delegates for Taft and 9 for Roosevelt. Almost all the Taft delegates were contested by Lyon, however, and the vote of Texas remained uncertain.[19]

The Ohio primary of May 21 was the climax of the entire pre-

16. C. W. Hornick to Hilles, March 6, 12, 1912, A. L. Shinn to Hilles, March 19, 1912, Hilles Papers.

17. J. R. Knowland to Hilles, April 26, 1912, Hilles Papers.

18. C. W. Hornick to Hilles, May 6, 1912, Hilles Papers.

19. H. F. MacGregor to Hilles, March 18, 23, April 16, 19, May 21, 28, 1912, J. B. Kealing to Hilles, May 20, 1912, Hilles Papers.

convention campaign. Taft men realized that a Roosevelt victory in the President's home state would be a damaging blow to the President's prestige. It might even supply Roosevelt with the necessary psychological boost to gain the nomination. A Taft victory, on the other hand, would go a long way toward revitalizing the President's campaign. In March Taft's position seemed relatively secure in his native state. Vorys told Hilles that Roosevelt was certain to capture only one of the twenty-one districts. The state central committee, controlled by the President's friends, met on March 30 and endorsed Taft for renomination.[20] State Chairman Lewis C. Laylin and State Committeeman Harry M. Daugherty perfected the regular organization during the first part of April. The President's brother Charles and nephew Hulbert managed the financial campaign. Carmi Thompson, the First Assistant Secretary of the Interior, and Ralph Tyler, the Auditor for the Navy Department, came from Washington as aides, while the Taft Bureau supplied campaign literature. Outside the regular organizations, the most important groups were businessmen's clubs for Taft in Cincinnati, Cleveland, and other large cities. After the Illinois and Pennsylvania primaries, the Taft men became very disturbed, and their pleas for speakers and money reached Washington daily. Chairman Laylin insisted by the end of the month that the President must make a speaking tour of the state.[21]

The Ohio campaign began on May 12 and lasted for eight days. Taft made two separate tours, traveled 3,000 miles, and spoke at over one hundred meetings. Repeatedly he denied charges brought by Roosevelt, and he defended his Administration without his customary reserve. Roosevelt, who traveled 1,750 miles and delivered seventy-five talks, attacked the President often and in abusive language. La Follette also campaigned in the primary, although he challenged in only seven congressional districts. The three campaign trains crisscrossed the state, missing one another in some towns by just a few moments. The pace was hectic. At one point the President's special did not stop as scheduled. All the workers from the Columbus Brick and Terra Cotta Company in Union Furnace, who had been let out to see Taft, could only watch the train whiz by.[22]

20. G. J. Karger to Hilles, March 27, 1912, L. C. Laylin to Taft, March 30, 1912, Taft to H. M. Daugherty, March 12, 1912, Hilles Papers.

21. L. C. Laylin to Hilles, April 9, 15, 17, 27, 1912, Hulbert Taft to Hilles, April 16, 1912, H. M. Daugherty to W. B. McKinley, April 16, 1912, C. A. Thompson to Hilles, April 17, 1912, Hilles Papers.

22. Pringle, *Taft*, II, 784; Warner, "Ohio's Crusade," 592; J. F. White to Hilles, May 9, 1912, Hilles Papers.

The Ohio primary was the most bitter of the campaigns in 1912. It left the President convinced that he must return to the sanctuary of impersonal and infrequent speeches for the remainder of the battle. Taft complained that public critics were all the same. First they criticized him for not answering Roosevelt; yet, he said, when he went into the fight, they made little distinction as to who was to blame for the unprecedented spectacle. "I have been through . . . an experience that I do not care to repeat."[23] The primary election returns were a sting to Taft's pride. Roosevelt won 34 delegates, Taft 8, and La Follette none. Taft's home county accounted for 4 of his delegates. Roosevelt carried sixty-nine of the eighty-eight counties, and his plurality over Taft was nearly 50,000 votes.

Following his defeat in the Ohio primary, Taft became more determined to gain the 6 delegates-at-large, which were to be chosen at a state convention on June 4. Still in no mood to accommodate progressives, the President wrote Vorys that he would not consider for a moment any suggestion of compromise. The votes involved, he said, were not necessary to his nomination. He could stand their loss and was even content to be beaten in the primary, but he could not yield any votes by agreement. "The principles that we represent are too important to the country to lose anything by our voluntary concession."[24] The President believed that it was necessary for the convention to adopt a sound state platform. Ohio regulars, on Vorys' advice, chose Warren G. Harding, the Republican gubernatorial candidate in 1910 and the owner of the Marion *Star*, to write the platform. "The editorials of the Marion Star," Vorys told Taft, "have been the equal of any paper you ever saw, both in substance and classic literature." Harding arrived in Washington on May 31, held a conference with Senator Burton on the contents of the platform, and returned with the Senator to Ohio in time for the convention.[25] The Taft men carried the state convention by 28 votes out of a total of 753. Their success was due largely to the fact that Senator Burton persuaded Maurice Maschke, the Republican leader in Cleveland, to deliver 48 votes from Cuyahoga County against the wishes of the delegation. The final division of national convention delegates in Ohio was 34 for Roosevelt and 14 for Taft.

Taft came through the pre-convention campaign with a slim majority

23. Taft to William Worthington, May 29, 1912, Taft Papers.
24. Taft to A. I. Vorys, May 30, 1912, Hilles Papers.
25. A. I. Vorys to Hilles, May 25, 1912, L. C. Laylin to Hilles, May 30, 1912, Hilles Papers.

of 37 delegates over all his opponents. Could he hold that lead at the convention? According to Hilles' calculations, Taft had 577 pledged delegates; Roosevelt had 450, and La Follette and Cummins had the remaining 51. Roosevelt was only 90 votes away from the majority of 540. Hilles and Taft were well aware that their lead could disappear, since

TABLE 7

RESULTS OF PRESIDENTIAL PRIMARIES

STATE	ROOSEVELT	TAFT	LA FOLLETTE	OTHERS
California	138,563	69,345	45,876	
Illinois	266,917	127,481	42,692	
Maryland	29,647	26,618	—	
Massachusetts	83,099	86,722	2,058	
Nebraska	46,795	13,241	16,785	
New Jersey	61,297	44,033	3,464	
North Dakota	23,669	1,876	34,123	
Ohio	165,809	118,362	15,570	
Oregon	28,905	20,517	22,491	
Pennsylvania	273,962	193,063	—	37,327
South Dakota	38,106	10,944	19,060	
Wisconsin	628	47,514	133,354	
TOTAL	1,157,397	761,716	351,043	

254 Taft delegates were in contest. Roosevelt unquestionably had a psychological edge. Would the delegates pledged to the President remain constant in the face of charges that Taft had manipulated his victories through patronage and fraud? Even if the President insisted on the falsity of these attacks, he could not deny that Roosevelt was the apparent choice of the rank and file. Roosevelt had an absolute majority over Taft and La Follette from twelve states which held direct primaries; he had gained the popular victory in nine states, La Follette in two, and Taft only in Massachusetts (see Table 7).[26] Before the first session of the national convention began on June 18, the President needed a favorable decision from the Republican National Committee on the contested delegates.

No one knew who would control the convention by the end of the first week in June. As part of the campaign of propaganda, each side counted as many as 600 votes on the first ballot. The Roosevelt camp claimed all contested delegates, and it appeared to the public that Roosevelt was in a better position than Taft. The Associated Press, which was supposed to be impartial, reported the following tabulation on June 10, only a

26. Victor Rosewater, *Back Stage in 1912* (Philadelphia, 1932), 119. As originally printed, the Taft total should read 759,716 and the La Follette 335,473.

week before the convention: instructed for Roosevelt and uncontested, 201; uninstructed, 166; contested, 254. The Republican National Committee, whose duty it was to hear contests and make up the temporary roll of the convention, became the object of national attention. Upon its decisions, in all probability, the final outcome of the convention would rest.

The regulars had planned their strategy for the national committee sessions in April and May. Victor Rosewater, who had been acting chairman since the death of John F. Hill of Maine, wrote each committeeman that, in view of the certainty of a large number of contests, it was vital to have a full attendence.[27] Hilles named Senator Dick to supervise the contests, while the President selected as counselors Samuel J. Elder, a Boston lawyer and his personal friend, and Foster V. Brown, a lawyer from Tennessee. Dick wrote to a leading Taft supporter in each state during May, requesting exact information about contested delegates, and for a month the Senator and his aides prepared testimony and legal briefs for the consideration of the committee. At the President's suggestion, Rosewater agreed to an open committee meeting. Taft told the acting chairman that he was in favor of impartiality and that he wanted no contest decided in his favor merely for the purpose of winning. The President was confident that the course of Roosevelt and Dixon had been such as to lend very little respectability to any of their claims. "It is important that the public should know that there are no star chamber proceedings and that they shall have access to the evidence upon which you act, through the newspapers."[28] The public was not invited, but the national committee asked ten representatives from five press associations and a stenographer to attend meetings.

Notices of 254 contested seats went through the committee hopper during a two-week session. In many cases the committee easily reached a decision. With rare exceptions, the crudely manufactured contests from the South, which accounted for more than one-third of the seats in dispute, collapsed of their own weight. Of the 107 southern delegates contested, the committee seated 101 by unanimous vote. The sessions were, nevertheless, filled with bitter debate. Governors Hadley and William R. Stubbs, Francis J. Heney of California, and William Flinn of Pittsburgh, the strategy board for Roosevelt, pressed their arguments forcefully. The leading Taft members of the committee, Crane, McKinley, and Butler, were equally adamant. The Taft men insisted that the hearings were fair

27. Victor Rosewater to Hilles, April 17, 30, 1912, Hilles Papers.
28. Taft to Rosewater, May 31, 1912, Hilles Papers.

and the contests decided on merit, while the Roosevelt members complained of fraud and theft.[29]

The committee as a whole was less interested in justice than in seating enough delegates pledged to Taft to insure his renomination. Employing partisan tactics, the committee awarded 235 contested delegates to Taft and only 19 to Roosevelt. Roosevelt probably had a right to almost 30 more delegates. These seats would not have given Roosevelt a majority of convention delegates, but, with the addition of delegates for Cummins and a few for La Follette, the Roosevelt forces would have been able to dictate the organization of the convention and to block Taft's victory on, at least the first ballot.[30] The closeness of the contest showed how vital was the Old Guard offensive in 1911. Without it Taft would have had neither the delegate strength nor the party machinery to manipulate his renomination.

Still hoping to overrule the action of the national committee, Roosevelt came to Chicago in a surprise move shortly before the convention opened. He announced that the committee fight would be taken to the convention floor. Speaking in scathing terms, Roosevelt denounced the Republican National Committee and the President. If the convention failed to seat 76 of his contesting delegates, Roosevelt said, and as a result Taft became the nominee, his supporters would not endorse the ticket.

The Taft men had anticipated a contest on the convention floor and were prepared to select convention officers who were friendly to the President. The regulars began in April to consider seriously who would best qualify for the position of temporary chairman. Former Governor Murphy of New Jersey thought the chairman should be a man accustomed to presiding, familiar with parliamentary law, quick of perception, and above all of undaunted resolution—"in short a man who by his strength of character would give weight to his decisions."[31] The subcommittee on arrangements considered President Nicholas Murray Butler of Columbia University, former Governor John William Griggs of New Jersey, and Senator Charles E. Townsend of Michigan among others. Harry New, chairman of the subcommittee, and Senator Crane both favored Senator Root, and on May 18 New wired Root that the subcommittee wished to appoint him chairman. The next day New tele-

29. S. J. Elder to Hilles, June 12, 1912, Hilles Papers; N. M. Butler to Taft, June 24, 1912, Taft Papers.
30. Taft to William Worthington, May 29, 1912, Taft Papers; Taft to Hilles, June 11, 1912, Hilles Papers.
31. Franklin Murphy to Hilles, April 15, 1912, Hilles Papers.

graphed the President, "I trust you will urge him to notify me of his acceptance at once."[32] Root had written to Taft on May 15, saying he could not bring himself to speak on questions between Taft and Roosevelt. His fighting days were over, he said. He was sixty-seven and would soon step aside for younger men. But there was little room for neutrals. The press published the story that Root had been asked to preside, and the Senator accepted thereafter.[33]

Once the committee had selected Root as temporary chairman, William Barnes of New York began to enlist delegates for his support. "The fight should be concentrated on Root as the only way to get control of the convention," Barnes said.[34] He wrote to Taft delegates throughout the country, advising them that the Roosevelt forces would oppose Senator Root. In behalf of the New York delegation, Barnes requested a collect wire from each delegate indicating his vote for Root as temporary chairman.[35] Many assurances of support reached Taft headquarters, particularly from southern chairmen. A typical reply was that of State Chairman Remmel, who promised that the Arkansas delegation would be a "solid phalanx."[36] Approximately at this time, Taft agreed with Hilles that Barnes should be named the floor manager at the convention in order to "stiffen the backbone" of some delegates. In addition, Hilles appointed men as secretaries, doorkeepers, and sergeants at arms, who were "quick on their feet, absolutely loyal, and experienced politicians, with such dispositions that they will not be carried away by the stampede that will be attempted."[37]

The Taft organization tried to control the visitor's gallery as well as the convention floor. The demand for tickets was the greatest that Harry New had ever known in his many years of experience. The rumor circulated in the Taft camp that the Roosevelt people were begging the greater share of the tickets to the convention, and that they had started an organized movement to pack the gallery in order to stampede the convention. The national committee distibuted tickets generally in a fair manner, but New followed the precedent that former Presidents should

32. H. S. New to Hilles, April 8, 26, 1912, and to Taft, May 19, 1912, Hilles Papers.
33. W. M. Crane to Hilles, May 15, 1912, Hilles Papers.
34. William Barnes to Taft, May 30, 1912, Taft Papers.
35. William Barnes to I. M. Ullman, May 28, 1912, Hilles Papers.
36. H. L. Remmel to Hilles, May 31, 1912, Hilles Papers.
37. William Barnes to Hilles, May 30, 1912, J. C. Eversman to W. B. McKinley, April (n.d.), 1912, Hilles Papers; William Barnes to Taft, May 30, 1912, Taft Papers.

receive no extra tickets to a convention and did not allot tickets for Roosevelt's personal use. The Roosevelt boosters charged that the Taft managers were plotting a covert scheme to fill the Coliseum with the President's friends.[38]

The first session of the convention began on June 18 with a brief debate about the contests which set the stage for the selection of a temporary chairman. The Taft forces nominated Root, while the Roosevelt organization nominated Governor Francis E. McGovern of Wisconsin for the chairmanship. Roosevelt had decided upon McGovern in the hope that a Wisconsin man would gain the support of La Follette's delegates. In the first significant vote of the convention, the Taft forces held firm and Root was elected by 57 votes over McGovern. The final result of the convention was a foregone conclusion thereafter: the Taft organization was in control.

The emotions of the Roosevelt supporters burst loose during the second day of the convention. Governor Hadley presented a motion to replace 72 contested Taft delegates with Roosevelt men. In the debate the young, good-looking governor handled himself with confidence and calmness. The Roosevelt delegates, who had been sitting on hard chairs, without food, drink, or cigars for four hours, cheered him loudly. The Roosevelt managers, who had been awaiting such an opportunity, artfully manipulated the clamor into a demonstration, and the delirium of one Roosevelt delegate affected another. "They became like dancing dervishes . . . at a negro camp-meeting who have found religion." In rhythmic yells they called, "We want Teddy! We want Teddy!" The California delegation, waving flags, handkerchiefs, and newspapers, led a march through the aisles. As the excitement of the sweating enthusiasts waned after half an hour, a young lady, apparently on a cue from the Roosevelt managers, leaned over the balcony and waved a poster on which was a likeness of Roosevelt. She delivered a speech, flailing her arms in the air, pointing at the portrait, shaking her fist at the Taft delegates and throwing kisses to the Roosevelt men. Several men from the California delegation rushed to the gallery and escorted the young lady to the floor. Against the protests of the sergeants at arms, they hoisted her atop the reporters' tables, where she continued her speech. The demonstration renewed and the tumult rose to a fever pitch. Finally the Roosevelt delegates, sitting in quiet exhaustion, voted on Hadley's motion. The motion was tabled 567 to 507 and referred to the

38. H. S. New to Hilles, May 20, 28, 1912, J. C. Eversman to W. B. McKinley, April (n.d.), 1912, Hilles Papers.

committee on credentials, where the permanent roll was to be adopted.[39]

The action of the committee on credentials was only a repetition of the decisions made by the national committee. After the report on the permanent roll was delivered and accepted on the last day of the convention, Henry J. Allen of Kansas read a message from Roosevelt. Roosevelt said that the national committee had stolen 80 or 90 delegates for Taft and defeated the will of the people. Since the convention refused to purge the roll, it no longer represented the party. Indeed, the convention was a fraud, and anyone accepting its nominees would forfeit the right to ask the support of honest men.

Most of the Roosevelt delegates sat in silent protest on the last day of the convention, refusing to leave, but remaining apart from the proceedings. Warren Harding placed the President's name before the convention. Taft received 561 votes, only 16 shy of Hilles' pre-convention estimate; 107 delegates voted for Roosevelt, and 349 recorded themselves as present but not voting (6, including Governor Johnson of California, had left the Coliseum). The other 41 delegates divided their votes between La Follette, Cummins, and Hughes. The vice-presidential nomination, which followed immediately, was just a formality. Roosevelt rejected a movement to name Hadley as a compromise candidate, and Vice-President Sherman was renominated without contest despite the fact that he was suffering from a severe heart ailment.[40]

Roosevelt resolved the question of whether his supporters should bolt the Republican party at a meeting just after the convention. He declared that the contest was one which could not be settled along party lines. Roosevelt asked the delegates to return home in order to ascertain the sentiment of the people, and then to assemble in a mass convention, where they could nominate a progressive candidate on a progressive platform. Except for the formality of a second convention, the party was split at last.

Thus the President's early drive for party control paid its dividends

39. R. H. Davis, "The Two Conventions at Chicago," *Scribner's Magazine,* LII (September, 1912), 265-69; Rosewater, *Back Stage,* 179-80; *Fifteenth Republican National Convention: Official Report of the Proceedings* (New York, 1912), 143, 160.

40. "I knew I needed a rest," Sherman said, "but it was not until I went into the Adirondacks in June and the altitude aggravated my ailment that I suspected that it was the heart muscles that had become weakened. That is the difficulty however and my breathing is so labored that it takes me 3 to 5 minutes to go upstairs. The first 3 weeks of July I was not permitted to take part in the campaign at any time. . . ." Sherman died on October 30. J. S. Sherman to Hilles, September 4, 1912, Hilles Papers.

at the June convention. In the face of Roosevelt's enormous popularity, and despite a well-organized progressive drive in 1912, Taft won renomination. Unable to achieve their aims within Republicanism, Roosevelt and many of his supporters formed the Progressive party in August. Taft's uncompromising spirit, Hilles' skillful manipulation of the Old Guard, and the progressive bolt led many reformers out of the Republican party at just the time when they threatened to control it.

With the conservatives alone in command of the party, Taft was hopeful about the future of Republicanism. Yet he did not look forward with any enthusiasm to the final weeks of the campaign. The President fully expected Woodrow Wilson, the Democratic candidate, to win on November 5. Taft's main objectives in the national campaign were to defeat Roosevelt and to hold the Old Guard forces in line for conservative victories in the future. In order to do this, Taft was entirely willing to let the Republican party be made smaller for the time being.[41]

41. Taft to Horace Taft, November 1, 1912, Hilles Papers.

5. VICTORY IN DEFEAT

The post-convention period was an anticlimax to the contest for nomination. The campaign mirrored Taft's view that his hour of personal triumph had passed when he forced Roosevelt out of the party. "With the great satisfaction in having accomplished that which to me and to the country was the most important thing, to wit, the defeat of Theodore Roosevelt," Taft wrote, "I can look forward to any result now with very considerable satisfaction, whether it leads me out of the White House or keeps me there four more years."[1]

At the insistence of the President, Hilles became the chairman of the Republican National Committee in July, with the Taft organization operating much as it had in the pre-convention campaign. While the President remained in Washington, Hilles established his headquarters in New York and appointed new officers to the Taft Bureau in Chicago, including David W. Mulvane, of Kansas, as director and Walter H. Wilson, a Chicago banker, as treasurer.

In contrast with previous election campaigns, the Republicans found money hard to obtain. As soon as he assumed the chairmanship, Hilles became sorely pressed to meet expenses. He also had an exasperating experience in filling the post of treasurer. George R. Sheldon declined to continue, and in succession seven other men refused to serve. After nearly five weeks in his New York headquarters, Hilles could not find a man to replace Sheldon. During the last part of August Sheldon finally agreed to retain the office, providing that Franklin Q. Brown of New York would share the duties and responsibilities. Sheldon could not solve the financial plight of the Republicans any more than Hilles. Part of the difficulty was that many who had contributed large amounts to the pre-convention campaign refused to reach again into their purses. Hilles kept the total post-convention campaign expenditures to about $800 thousand, a figure far below some of the previous campaigns, which usually reached $2 million and sometimes $3 million.[2]

The Republican campaign was unexciting. Taft retired from the stump and delivered a few calm speeches in which he defended his Administration, constitutional government, and an independent judici-

1. Taft to G. H. Earle, July 9, 1912, Hilles Papers.
2. Hilles to Henry Taft, August 1, 1912, W. H. Wilson to Hilles, September 11, October 11, 1912, Hilles Papers.

ary. The campaign stressed the traditional benefits of a Republican administration to the nation. Prosperity, tariff protection for businessmen and workers, individual liberty for all groups regardless of background, and justice for all under the guarantees of the Constitution were the major points of the appeal for Taft's re-election.

In the main, regular leaders devoted their post-convention energies to strengthening Old Guard organizations. Throughout the country Taft withheld patronage appointments until November in order to keep federal appointees loyal to the Administration, while regulars forced Roosevelt men to declare themselves for the Progressive party.

Old Guard leaders also fought strenuously against a movement to compromise the electoral ticket. A number of Republicans, more concerned with local victory over the Democrats than with the success of the national ticket, sponsored an electoral plan. They proposed to place the same electors under the names of both Roosevelt and Taft, with the understanding that in each state the electors would vote for the man having the highest total of popular votes. Progressives attempted to carry out the proposal for identical electors in nineteen states, although Roosevelt refused to have anything to do with the scheme. Taft was absolutely opposed to any attempt to eradicate clear lines between the Republicans and the Progressives.[3]

For weeks the Taft organization worked at Republican state conventions and committee meetings, or through legal proceedings and the threat of court action, to secure a complete separation of the electoral ticket. The Old Guard thereby removed seventy-three Roosevelt electors from the Republican ticket and provided a clear test of popularity between Taft and Roosevelt in every state except South Dakota and California.

The November election was a defeat for the Republican party, as expected. Taft's popular vote was about 3.5 million, while Roosevelt gained more than 4 million votes and Wilson won over 6 million. Taft carried just two states. In Vermont the President edged Roosevelt by 1,000 votes; in Utah a Gentile-Mormon coalition, led by Senator Smoot against a Catholic senatorial rival, was just strong enough to provide Taft with a plurality of 6,000 over Wilson. Roosevelt won in six states and Wilson in forty. This gave Wilson 435 electoral votes, Roosevelt 88, and Taft 8.

The election returns convinced a number of Republicans that the party had to be reorganized on a progressive basis. Governor Hadley,

3. Taft to Hilles, August 7, 1912, Hilles Papers.

Senators Cummins and Kenyon, Congressman Parsons, and Secretary Stimson began taking quiet steps immediately after the election to recruit Bull Moosers into the Republican party. Late in November Hadley proposed that the national committee should call a Republican convention within six months to consider presidential primaries and a reapportionment of southern delegates. "I believe," Hadley said, "a very considerable portion, if not a majority, of those who left the Republican party will return to it if they can feel assured that within the party in the future the will of the majority will control. . . ."[4]

Old Guardsmen, on the other hand, thought that the election indicated a secure future in American politics for conservative Republicanism. The November returns showed that the Republican party still had a national appeal. While Taft carried no state by a majority, Roosevelt won a clear lead only where there was no Republican ticket—in California and South Dakota. Although the Republican vote was small, it was not sectional. Taft had a lead over Roosevelt and Wilson in counties scattered throughout the nation. In both the cities and rural areas Taft did equally well, polling about 25 per cent of the vote. The Democrats in 1912 failed to win a significant portion of the normally Republican electorate. Indeed, Wilson ran behind Bryan's count in 1908 by more than 120,000. He gained a majority only in the traditionally Democratic South and in the new state of Arizona. Roosevelt received some Democratic votes as well as the major share of Republican defectors, but the Progressive party nevertheless did not fare well. Although the Progressives offered a full ticket in a majority of states, they captured just one governorship, about twelve congressmen, and approximately 250 of over 1,000 local offices. Roosevelt generally exceeded the vote for other Bull Moose candidates by 20 to 50 per cent; without him there was virtually no Progressive party.

The President saw nothing in the voting statistics to change his pre-election attitudes about progressives. Roosevelt's popular vote was a personal disappointment to Taft, but otherwise the President was content with the results. Taft felt that in time, when progressives became hungry for office, they would return to Republicanism on Old Guard terms. He thought it would not hurt "our Republican friends to have their noses rubbed in the mud. They have been so smug . . . and so dis-

4. H. S. Hadley to Taft, November 18, 1912, Taft Papers; Hadley to N. M. Butler, November 21, 1912, Nicholas Murray Butler Papers, Columbia University Library; H. L. Stimson to Hadley, November 11, 1912, and to L. C. Griscom, December 5, 1912, Stimson Papers.

posed to kick at and criticise everybody and everything that they might as well get a lesson in adversity." The President was not worried about Wilson and the Democratic party: "They never miss an opportunity, having power, to hari-kari." Taft predicted that the Democrats might last more than one term, but they certainly would not last more than two.[5]

With the consent of his Old Guard advisers, therefore, the President rejected Hadley's proposal. The principles of the Republican party, Taft said, were much more important than the membership of the next convention. Presidential primaries and southern representation could be attended to when the time came. The President was concerned lest there be any compromise which would give Roosevelt some power in the party to push his "pernicious principles" of constitutional limitations. In order to retain the spirit of true Republicanism, Taft maintained, the party had to oppose judicial recall and uphold the Constitution.[6]

The attitude of the President and his Old Guard associates reflected their view that the Republican party could rehabilitate itself without Roosevelt and those who agreed with his doctrines. The regulars knew that 3.5 million people had stayed with the Republicans under the most unfavorable circumstances. Hilles and Butler also believed that at least 1.5 million Republicans, who wanted to defeat Roosevelt, had either stayed at home or had voted for Wilson. In addition, the Old Guard leaders thought that another 2 million, who had voted for Roosevelt because of temporary dissatisfaction, would return to the party. Thus Old Guardsmen reasoned that there were about 7 million conservative voters with whom to work in a rebuilding process.[7]

Since Taft felt that his practical usefulness as party leader would diminish greatly after his term of office, he called on Hilles to captain the Old Guard organization for the next four years. The President was confident that Hilles had the experience to withstand progressive pressures for party change. "Your headship of the National Committee is such as to retain you in close relation with the politics of the country," the President told his secretary, "and whatever you do I will approve because I know you will do it only after the most careful thought." Taft turned his own attention to a study of constitutional and governmental

5. Taft to C. H. Clark, November 8, 1912, Hilles Papers.
6. Taft to C. H. Clark, November 8, 1912, and to Herbert Parsons, November 20, 1912, Hilles Papers; Taft to Parsons, November 21, 1912, Taft Papers.
7. N. M. Butler to Taft, December 16, 1912, Butler Papers; Butler to Hilles, December 16, 1912, Hilles, "The Future of the Republican Party" (manuscript, 1913), 3-10, Hilles Papers.

law in preparation for his teaching post at the Yale law school. The President thought that the demands for initiative, referendum, and the recall of judicial decisions were alien to the American system of government. He also believed that American universities were becoming the "seed-plots of socialism." As a professor of law Taft hoped to do his part "to clarify the atmosphere in our academic lecture rooms so that the young men should not come out of college callow socialists but staunch supporters of representative government."[8]

Certain that Republicanism could stand temporary defeat, Hilles played a waiting game as chairman. He refused to call the national committee into extraordinary session or to reorganize the party structure. If Old Guardsmen yielded to any socialistic proposition, Hilles said, or if they accepted progressives as Republican leaders, the party would greatly impair its power for usefulness. The Republican party was too strongly intrenched locally as a political organization to be driven out of politics, Hilles maintained; this was not true of the Progressive party. "The Progressive party was born in a passion and lived in excitement that cannot be maintained permanently," Hilles said, "and the natural tendency under normal conditions is for the average Republican, who left the party in 1912 in order to vote for Mr. Roosevelt, to return to it."[9]

President Taft's renomination was, then, primarily the result of his own initiative and long-range planning. After he directed Hilles to organize the forces of regular Republicanism in the spring of 1911, Taft gained two important political assets. Personally the President became a more confident politician, whose Old Guard partisanship did not alter greatly before progressive attacks. Tactically he acquired a disciplined national organization before any progressive leaders announced their presidential availability. Without his determination and an early lead in the contest for convention delegates, Taft probably would have lost the nomination.

Although Roosevelt entered the campaign at a disadvantage, he had a great impact on Republican politics. Within a month of his presidential announcement, Roosevelt's organizations were operating efficiently. From the middle of April progressives made sweeping inroads into Taft's delegate lead, and Hilles' work became more difficult. A number of regular leaders abandoned the President's cause in order to maintain power in

8. Taft to C. H. Clark, November 8, 1912, and to Hilles, April 25, 1913, Hilles Papers.
9. Hilles, "The Future," 12-13, 42, Hilles Papers.

74

their local organizations. Old Guard factionalism became so severe that Hilles in several states failed entirely to unite the regular organizations behind the President.

The general effect of Roosevelt's campaign, however, was to drive Taft and the Old Guard into closer association. The former President's doctrines and his threat to Old Guard political power alarmed conservatives. For most regulars there was no choice but to support Taft. Convinced for months that his success depended on cooperation with the Old Guard, Taft only reinforced his reliance on the regulars when Roosevelt became a candidate. After progressive primary victories in April, Taft campaigned with greater personal intensity, but he did not change his direction. The President remained constant in his desires to achieve renomination and to preserve conservatism in the Republican party.

Roosevelt's candidacy and bolt completed the Republican schism and gave a new lease of life to the party's conservatives. Regulars cared little about charges that Taft had stolen the nomination. Breaking few rules or precedents, the regulars felt that they had engineered the party by the same devices Roosevelt employed in 1904 and 1908. When Roosevelt formed a party outside their ranks, most Old Guardsmen were pleased. As Taft expressed it, the Bull Moose convention in August contained a conglomeration of radical elements which the Republican party was well rid of.[10] The Old Guard forces lost the election of 1912, but they held their grip on party organization, and came through the period of insurgency in victory.

10. Taft to Hilles, August 7, 1912, Hilles Papers.

UNIVERSITY OF FLORIDA MONOGRAPHS

Social Sciences

No. 1 (Winter 1959): *The Whigs of Florida, 1845-1854*. By Herbert J. Doherty, Jr.

No. 2 (Spring 1959): *Austrian Catholics and the Social Question, 1918-1933*. By Alfred Diamant

No. 3 (Summer 1959): *The Siege of St. Augustine in 1702*. By Charles W. Arnade

No. 4 (Fall 1959): *New Light on Early and Medieval Japanese Historiography*. By John A. Harrison

No. 5 (Winter 1960): *The Swiss Press and Foreign Affairs in World War II*. By Frederick H. Hartmann

No. 6 (Spring 1960): *The American Militia: Decade of Decision, 1789-1800*. By John K. Mahon

No. 7 (Summer 1960): *The Foundation of Jacques Maritain's Political Philosophy*. By Hwa Yol Jung

No. 8 (Fall 1960): *Latin American Population Studies*. By T. Lynn Smith

No. 9 (Winter 1961): *Jacksonian Democracy on the Florida Frontier*. By Arthur W. Thompson

No. 10 (Spring 1961): *Holman Versus Hughes: Extension of Australian Commonwealth Powers*. By Conrad Joyner

No. 11 (Summer 1961): *Welfare Economics and Subsidy Programs*. By Milton Z. Kafoglis

No. 12 (Fall 1961): *Tribune of the Slavophiles: Konstantin Aksakov*. By Edward Chmielewski

No. 13 (Winter 1962): *City Managers in Politics: An Analysis of Manager Tenure and Termination*. By Gladys M. Kammerer, Charles D. Farris, John M. DeGrove, and Alfred B. Clubok

No. 14 (Spring 1962): *Recent Southern Economic Development as Revealed by the Changing Structure of Employment*. By Edgar S. Dunn, Jr.

No. 15 (Summer 1962): *Sea Power and Chilean Independence*. By Donald E. Worcester

No. 16 (Fall 1962): *The Sherman Antitrust Act and Foreign Trade*. By Andre Simmons

No. 17 (Winter 1963): *The Origins of Hamilton's Fiscal Policies*. By Donald F. Swanson

No. 18 (Spring 1963): *Criminal Asylum in Anglo-Saxon Law*. By Charles H. Riggs, Jr.

No. 19 (Summer 1963): *Colonia Barón Hirsch, A Jewish Agricultural Colony in Argentina*. By Morton D. Winsberg

No. 20 (Fall 1963): *Time Deposits in Present-Day Commercial Banking*. By Lawrence L. Crum

No. 21 (Winter 1964): *The Eastern Greenland Case in Historical Perspective*. By Oscar Svarlien

No. 22 (Spring 1964): *Jacksonian Democracy and the Historians*. By Alfred A. Cave

No. 23 (Summer 1964): *The Rise of the American Chemistry Profession, 1850-1900*. By Edward H. Beardsley

No. 24 (Fall 1964): *Aymara Communities and the Bolivian Agrarian Reform*. By William E. Carter

No. 25 (Winter 1965): *Conservatives in the Progressive Era: The Taft Republicans of 1912*. By Norman M. Wilensky